D0342134

▼▼▼▼

SAVORY
SOUTHWEST

▲▲▲▲▲

SAVORY SOUTHWEST

PRIZE-WINNING
RECIPES FROM THE
ARIZONA REPUBLIC

by Judy Hille Walker

Illustrated by Monte Varah

Northland Publishing

TO LUCILE TROWER,
who taught me to appreciate good food.

Copyright © 1990 by Phoenix Newspapers Inc.

All Rights Reserved

This book may not be reproduced in whole or in part, by any means (with the exception of short quotes for the purpose of review), without the permission of the publisher. For information, address Northland Publishing Co., P.O. Box 1389, Flagstaff, Arizona 86002.

FIRST EDITION
THIRD PRINTING 1993

Library of Congress Catalog Card Number 89-63748

Manufactured in Hong Kong
Cataloging in Publication Data
Walker, Judy Hille.
    Savory Southwest : prize- winning recipes from the
    Arizona Republic/by Judy Hille Walker ; illustrated
    by Monte Varah.—1st ed.
    ISBN 0-87358-501-1
    1. Cookery, American—Southwestern style.
1. Arizona republic. II. Title.
TX715.2.S69W35   1990
    641.5979—dc20   89-63748
                        CIP

CONTENTS

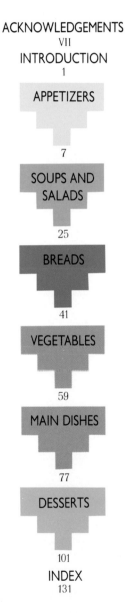
Note: The sections are color-coded for your convenience.
Look for the corresponding color on each page.

ACKNOWLEDGEMENTS

So many people at Phoenix Newspapers Inc. were vital parts of the recipe contests through the years. Many are unsung heros, such as the people on the *Republic's* features copy desk; these devoted journalists never get their names in the paper, but time and again they rescue those of us who do. On tight deadlines, they ground their way through recipes — once, twice, three times — checking and rechecking to be sure the things were as correct as possible before they saw print. Special thanks to all of them, past and present, including Jane E. Allen, Sal Caputo, Cathy Coggins, Sylvia Cody, Mark Hein, Dave Michaels, Gary Olmstead, Linda Vachata, Dave Gianelli, Gary Olson, Larry Rodgers and Cindy Zirwes.

PNI has one of the best Promotions and Public Relations departments in the business, and it was always a joy to work with them. These people know how to stage an event, and the outcome was always a delight for our contestants. Cindy Yomantas, David Hume, Natasha Lazutin, Joann Hurley, Veronica Mier, Donna Martinez, Grace Wood, many talented artists and a cheerful support staff devoted countless hours to the recipe contests, and made it all fun.

Then there were the people in *Republic* features who had a hand in the contest year after year. Mike McKay deserves credit for overseeing the recipe special sections, and for being a terrific editor, manager and friend. Anita Mabante Leach was, at times singlehandedly, responsible for the appetizing, appealing and surprising cover designs and food photos that graced our pages for years. This woman hauled uncounted bushels of groceries to photo studios, and every year she spent a fall Saturday assisting photographers at the recipe contest. Anita made us all look good, and I will be ever-grateful for her talent and friendship.

Special mention must go to Elin Jeffords, who rounded up and sat with our distinguished final judges at the contests, and who helped me sort, read and evaluate all 2,200 recipes in 1988. Other feature-department folk who made contributions above and beyond the call of duty through the years were Jim Cook, Tom Bauer, Gail Tabor, Charlie Sanders, Julie Newberg, Jean Novotny, Dorothee Polson and Jacquie Dean.

Contest photographers deserve special credit for hard work under difficult conditions: Tom Story, Sean Brady, Michael Meister, Suzanne Starr, Mike Fioritto, Ken Akers, David Barr. The recipe tabloids were also consistently well-illustrated by *Republic* artists Patti Valdez, Kee Rash and Matt Nielsen.

Outside 120 East Van Buren, countless people in the food community generously gave their time to serve as judges, screening the recipes and tasting the final results. To all of them we are grateful, including Kresent Thuringer, Barbara Fenzl, Sylvia Smith, Linda Vaughn, Chris Gross, Eric Denk, Sarah Labensky, Ray Vincenzio, Jon McCabe, Martha Kain, Linda Marcinko, Erasmo Kamnitzer, Karen Close, Laurie Vacha, Lenard Rubin, Michael Whitesides, Gunther Landinger, Larry Long, Joe Ball, Werner Fehr, Larry Grucky, Rene Jacobus, Ken Yoshimura, Armand Chavez, Hans Glauser, Dave Linhart, Albert Stadeli, Michael Zyla, Ludwig Strodel and Guy Rochelle. (I regret that I cannot find complete records of screening judges through the years, because those people worked especially hard to winnow all the recipes submitted down to just a few finalists.)

My personal thanks for assistance in putting this book together must go to Susan McDonald of Northland Publishing, whose idea it was; to computer wizards Howie Fischer, Sam Dillingham and Charlie Walker; to my in-laws Beverly and Charles Walker for hours of babysitting; and to my parents Bill and Bobbie Trower for the same. Bobbie Jo Trower, Vera Walker and Kim MacEachern helped me test recipes. Dave Walker, my husband, provided endless support, taste-testing and editing advice. Mack provided precious smiles.

Finally, my heartfelt gratitude to the readers of *The Arizona Republic* Food section, and all those who ever contributed to Recipe Round Table or entered a recipe contest. You were the reason it all happened.

JUDY HILLE WALKER

INTRODUCTION

This book is a compilation of the best and most popular recipes from the seven cooking contests sponsored by *The Arizona Republic* Food section in the 1980s. Each contest had a different theme: Movable Feasts; Just Desserts; Taste of Arizona; Healthy Appetites; Festive Favorites; Zest of the Southwest; Easy Entertaining. All recipes were previously printed in special sections inserted in Sunday newspapers.

The contests were always a lot of fun, for the finalists as well as those of us who sponsored them. On the big day when the taste-offs were held, five people won money, all the finalists got a prize of some sort and everybody went home happy. But the process didn't end then, because the recipes were published. Their utility is on-going.

The foods you will find in this book range from simple to sophisticated. The common thread is that they all came from readers, people who had a good recipe and decided — often on a whim — to enter it in a contest. If there was one thing we heard contestants say over and over through the years, it was, "I didn't ever think I'd win."

The Arizona Republic held the first recipe contest in 1981. The location was the private park for *Republic* and *Gazette* employees, on East Indian School Road in Phoenix. At that time, the park still went by its original name, The Lazy R&G Ranch. (It's now known as The Ranch.) Twenty-four finalists, picked from a field of 1,144 by home economists on the basis of their written recipes, brought guests and their prepared dishes to the Ranch. Brunch was served in the outdoor pavilion. Several contestants and their kids rode Mr.

Train. Professional chefs judged Laurel Thompson's Ham Pinwheels, a three-ingredient appetizer, to be the grand prize winner. Laurel went home with a check for $500, and the recipe taste-off was deemed a great success.

After that, contests were held every fall except 1985. And I was lucky enough to be there for all of them. Through the years, working with our talented promotions team and *Republic* feature staffers, I got to do just about every job available, from setting up tables in the room where the cooks would work the next day to writing copy for the cover of the Food page. Phoning contestants to tell them they were eligible to come to the finals was one of my favorite duties — I was almost as excited as the person on the other end of the line.

Many of those people stand out in my mind, along with their dishes, which you will find in the following pages. At that first contest, which had the theme Movable Feasts, John Ullmschneider of Lake Havasu City brought his Encore Dip centered in a blue-and-white lifesaver, claiming he served it to guests that way in his pool.

In 1986, Catharine Calk McCarty brought her Kentucky Sweet Potatoes to the Festive Favorites finals. At 102, she was the contest's oldest finalist. Patricia Lapezio came from La Mesa, California, to compete in the 1987 Zest of the Southwest contest, and she stayed at the Scottsdale home of her sister, Peggy Milholland. They were both finalists in the desserts category — and they both made cheesecakes. This wild coincidence wasn't the end of it, either. In 1988, Patricia made the trip again, when her Cheesy Seafood Lasagna Rolls were among the dishes tasted by the final judges at the Easy Entertaining contest. Of course, Peggy came to cheer her sister on.

We learned that the unexpected will always happen. One year, 1983, we had an out-of-state grand prize winner, Michele Broadbent of Provo, Utah. She had the most Arizona-ish recipe in the very popular Just Desserts contest. Then there was the year a weed won. In 1982, Alicia Jacobs intrigued the judges with her Verdolagas recipe. She picked the round-leafed main ingredient out of her back yard. Results of the contest were always announced in the paper as quickly as possible, so as soon as the judges picked the grand prize winner, copy editors working in the features department that Saturday at the *Republic* scrambled into action with botany books. Before the day was over, they identified verdolagas in English as purslane, and learned that it had a long and distinguished culinary history as a wild and cultivated green.

That year's theme, A Taste of Arizona, made the contest particularly colorful. Joan Gordon was a finalist with a recipe developed by her husband, Arizona Supreme Court Justice Frank X. Gordon. Raised in Kingman, Gordon recreated the Jalapeño Pickled Eggs he had eaten in a bar in Grasshopper Junction, north of Kingman on U.S. Highway 93. (In 1988, Gordon became a household name as he presided over the impeachment trial of Arizona Governor Evan Mecham.)

Another 1982 entrant was Winona Talayumptewa, of Riviera, who brought Hopi bavaul-piki, known as blue balls. The marble-size dumplings of blue-corn flour have been made by Hopis for generations. And a Navajo recipe from that year remains the all-time most unusual dish ever brought to the contest: tamales made with sheeps' blood. The judges said it was similar to Scottish haggis. (Asked what might substitute for the sheeps' blood, the contestant suggested blood from a goat.)

Several fine cooks were finalists in more than one contest. Nancy Gerczynski of Phoenix won the grand prize in 1984 and nearly won it again in 1987 with her healthy, contemporary creations. Prescott resident Margaret Rhodes, who has an Italian background and a superb talent for unusual flavor combinations, was an early two-time, desserts-category winner.

In 1988, the recipe contest had the theme Easy Entertaining. More than 2,200 entries were winnowed down to 24 finalists. For the first time, the contest left The Ranch. The public was able to attend the event, and a crowd at MetroCenter watched when Carolyn Ness of Gilbert won the grand prize for her Sweet Potato Jalapeño Soup. Ness had never entered a recipe contest before, and she won $1,000 for her trouble.

If it sounds from the foregoing that the recipes here are loaded with jalapeños, please let me correct that impression. In selecting the dishes to be included in this cookbook, I did lean heavily towards creations with Mexican and Southwestern slants. There are also recipes here with roots in the South, a chicken salad from Vietnam and a cheese ball from Maui, to name a few examples. Through the years, however, we simply had more dishes with an Arizona taste. Good cooks use common ingredients in creative ways, so it is natural for Arizonans to experiment with area favorites such as green chilies, tequila, dates, jicama and tomatillos. But be assured that none of the recipes is going to incinerate your taste buds. Seasonings are generally along Sonoran lines, full of flavor, not fire. I think the hottest dish our judges ever tasted was the 1986 grand prize winner, Eric's Lucky Black-Eyed Peas—and creator Eric Gironda learned to make the dish where he grew up, in New Orleans.

As you cook your way through this book, you will encounter techniques as well as dishes specific to the Southwest. Roasting chilies is explained in Caldo de Queso y Chilie Verde, soup with cheese and green chilies. Want to make candy—from citrus peels—or extract the ruby juice of prickly pears? Instructions are included in recipes for Margarita Mousse and Prickly Pear Jelly. Breads of the West hold a certain fascination, and these, too, are covered. Ernie Startup's recipe for Sinkers, a sourdough biscuit, beautifully explains how to work with the "starter" beloved by pioneers. A recipe for Navajo Fry Bread, a recipe that was constantly requested when I was food editor, is included in the Main Dish chapter with the recipe for Navajo Tacos. And in the new Southwest, tortillas are fried into cups to hold savory or sweet fillings, as detailed in Dessert Tostada with Lime Cream (page 122).

As we worked on the contest, we at the *Republic* were constantly pleased and surprised at the exceptional imagination that readers showed in their entries. In the year of Just Desserts, Jo Ann Hill submitted her entry, a peach cobbler, on cassette—set to music and sung. We invited her to the contest as a special guest, and she told us she planned an album of recipes. One special Arizona recipe we printed in 1987 was also not a finalist, and nobody ever made it (as far as we know). But this would have been suitable Southwestern fare for Paul Bunyan when he dragged his pickaxe through northern Arizona to create the Grand Canyon. It was sent to us by Norman L. Smith.

DUST DEVIL SOUP

1 medium-size dust devil (Check Game and Fish department for legal season, size, license needed and area permit)
100 gallons Salt River water
1 cast-iron pot, 100 gallon size

Bait dust devil with freshly washed linens hung in back yard to dry. Wait approximately 15 to 20 minutes (average time) for dust devil to attack. Pull pre-rigged cord from inside house to wrap clothesline tightly around dust devil. Quickly run outside and dispatch it with baseball bat.

Field-dress dust devil by removing tin cans, stones, stray pets and any unwanted cactuses, greasewood, herbs or other undesirable matter. (When properly cleaned, dust devil carcass should contain only those morsels and herbs you deem appetizing.) Each dust devil will have its own unique flavor, depending on area traveled before capture.

Fill iron pot with Salt River water. Build fire around post (missionary-cannibal style) and heat to boiling. Stand dust devil on end, lift up and begin screwing it into pot counterclockwise (in Southern hemisphere, clockwise) until fully submerged. Put lid on and let simmer for 5 to 6 hours. Remove lid and serve in asbestos bowls.

Serves approximately 200 guests, depending on method used to tie them to the table.

Those of you who make and eat these special dishes are as much a part of *The Arizona Republic's* recipe contests as the readers who submitted these entries and who bravely brought these dishes for judging. To me, that's the beauty of recipe contests.

APPETIZERS

Appetizers and snacks are one of the most satisfying categories of food. Since they are served
before or instead of a meal, or at parties, they are
savored alone. Each bite-size bit can be enjoyed
as it is.

For the cook, they are fun to make and serve.
And in the late '80s and early '90s, as eating
habits fragment and fewer meals are eaten at
scheduled times, these types of dishes are com-
ing into their own.

One food item that came into prominence in
the 1980s was the chicken wing. This downright-
neglected poultry part was an overnight snack
sensation across the country, after the Buffalo
Chicken Wing was invented by a bar owner in
Buffalo, New York. Dan's Wings, the 1988
appetizer category winner, sauces wings with a
savory mixture of soy sauce, red wine, thyme,
garlic, filé gumbo powder and, of course, Tabasco
sauce.

This chapter also has a few recipes that defy
categorization. Prickly Pear Jelly, a state standard, just had to be included. You will also see
here two unusual and delicious non-alcoholic
drinks. Both were developed for the Easy Entertaining contest, when we added a beverages
competition for the first time.

For entertaining, many of the recipes in this
section can be made partially or completely
ahead of time, so your party and guests can still
have the most essential ingredient—your undi-
vided attention.

Ham Pinwheels

Laurel Thompson

Ham pinwheels—what a great recipe this is. Laurel Thompson was the grand prize winner at the first *Arizona Republic* recipe contest with this recipe, and nobody was more surprised than Laurel when she won. Since 1981, when Laurel introduced me to this dish, I have made it hundreds of times. On hot summer nights, I have been known to roll up ham and cream cheese and call it dinner.

There are endless variations to this recipe, and I'm sure you'll create many of your own. Here are a few to start: Add to the cream cheese chopped green chilies, chopped black olives, celery seed, dill weed or seasoning mixes such as Mrs. Dash. Or substitute something else for the green onion in the center, such as a stalk of asparagus, strips of pimiento or slices of red, yellow or green pepper. (Kids love these.)

▼▼▼▼▼▼▼▼▼▼▼▼▼▼▼▼▼▼▼

1 package ham lunch meat
1 package (3 1/2 ounces)
  cream cheese

Green onions (1 for each
  slice of ham)

Spread cream cheese on each piece of lunch meat. Cut onions the diameter of the meat. Place on edge of ham and roll the meat around the onion. Place the rolls on a dish and put into freezer for an hour, which will make them easier to slice. Remove and cut each roll into small wheels by slicing the roll into ¼" pieces. Keep refrigerated until serving time. Makes 4 to 6 servings.

Caliente Cheese Fritters

Kathleen Farren

These colorful fritters are lightened by egg whites and baking powder. The secret to making them is to remember that, for all fried foods, the hotter the oil, the less greasy the finished product. Make sure the oil has come to proper temperature by dripping a bit of batter into the skillet; if it browns quickly, the oil is hot enough. Don't crowd the skillet with too many fritters at a time, or the batter temperature will cool the oil. This recipe surfaced in 1987 in the Zest of the Southwest contest.

3 eggs, separated
2 cups corn, canned or fresh
1/2 teaspoon salt
1/4 teaspoon black pepper
1 teaspoon baking powder
3/4 cup flour
1 cup Cheddar cheese, finely
   shredded
1/2 cup canned green
   chilies, chopped

1/4 cup red bell pepper,
   chopped
1/4 cup onion, finely
   chopped
Oil for frying
OPTIONAL GARNISHES:
Salsa
Sour cream

Beat egg whites until stiff. Pour corn into a separate mixing bowl. Add to corn the beaten yolks, salt, pepper, baking powder, flour, cheese, chilies, red pepper and onion. Mix well with a wooden spoon or spatula. Gently fold in beaten egg whites.

Heat about 1″ of oil in skillet. When the oil gets hot, drop fritters by spoonfuls. Brown on both sides. Drain on paper towels. Serve with salsa and a dollop of sour cream on the side, if desired. Makes 8 to 10 appetizer servings.

Dan's Wings

Dan Robertson

While hanging out in a neighborhood joint waiting for an order of Buffalo chicken wings, Dan Robertson of Phoenix was told by another patron how his aunt down south prepared such things. Robertson thought it sounded so good that he went home and tinkered with the ingredients until he came up with this recipe, which won the category prize for him in the 1988 Easy Entertaining contest. Robertson told us he started cooking when he quit smoking a few years ago, and he asked his wife to translate "tbsp." and "tsp." in cookbooks to help him get started. (*Note*: The filé gumbo powder is powdered sassafras root, used to thicken gumbo. Look for it on the spice aisle or the specialty section of your supermarket.)

▼▼▼▼▼▼▼▼▼▼▼▼▼▼▼▼▼▼▼▼

25 chicken wings
1 tablespoon thyme
2 or 3 cloves of garlic,
  minced
2 tablespoons file gumbo
  powder
1 cup dark soy sauce
1 cup red wine
1 stick unsalted butter
Tabasco sauce

Cut the chicken wings into 3 pieces. Save tips for another use, or discard. Marinate the chicken wings in the thyme, paprika, garlic, filé gumbo powder, soy sauce and wine for at least 2 hours, preferably overnight. Drain wings of marinade. Place wings on a cookie sheet that is greased or lined with foil. Preheat oven to 350° and bake for 30 to 35 minutes.

Melt butter in wok or large pan and add as many tablespoons of Tabasco as you like: 2 tablespoons for mild; 3 to 5 for medium; 6 or more for lots of heat.

Toss wings in Tabasco mixture. Serve with a bleu cheese dressing for dip, along with celery or carrots. Makes 50 wings.

Maui Cheese Logs

Kathy S. Kral

Contrast this recipe with the one on page 20. Can you believe they are basically the same? This cheese log went Hawaiian in the 1986 Festive Favorites contest. Creator Kathy S. Kral of Phoenix said that the year she and her family spent the Christmas holidays in Hawaii, they went to many beautiful buffets and brunches. When she returned, she duplicated the tasty cheese balls they had at a New Year's party. The Grand Marnier was the secret ingredient.

▼▼▼▼▼▼▼▼▼▼▼▼▼▼▼▼▼▼▼▼

1 jar (7 ounces) macadamia nuts
2 packages (8 ounces each) cream cheese, softened
1/2 pound sharp Cheddar cheese, finely grated

3 teaspoons grated orange rind
6 tablespoons Grand Marnier liqueur

In food processor, chop macadamia nuts. Reserve 3 tablespoons and set aside. Place rest of chopped nuts in a medium-size bowl and add the cheeses. Blend. Add the orange rind and Grand Marnier. Blend well. Divide mixture in half and spoon each into a rectangle of plastic wrap. Fold wrap around mixture and form into logs. Refrigerate until firm. When ready to serve, remove plastic and sprinkle with remaining nuts. This can be frozen and gets tastier by the day. Makes two cheese logs, about a pound each.

Mexican Egg Rolls with Fresh Salsa

Susan Anderson

In the Zest of the Southwest contest in 1987, finalist Susan Anderson of Glendale said she was making Chinese egg rolls and was inspired to create a Mexican version for this contest. Her fresh salsa won praise from the judges for its spunk. It has two quintessential salsa ingredients—tomatillos and fresh cilantro—as well as a special preparation technique—turning the green chilies into a puree. All other ingredients are hand-chopped for the best texture.

▼▼▼▼▼▼▼▼▼▼▼▼▼▼▼▼▼▼▼▼

SALSA:
1/2 pound tomatillos,
   husked and washed
1 large tomato
1/2 medium onion
1 teaspoon fresh cilantro
1 can (3 1/2 or 4 ounces)
   chopped green chilies
1 tablespoon white wine
   vinegar
Salt to taste (if desired)

EGG ROLLS:
1/2 pound mild chorizo
1/2 medium onion, finely
   chopped
1 cup refried beans
1 cup Monterey Jack
   cheese shredded
1/4 teaspoon ground cumin
1/8 teaspoon cayenne
   pepper
24 won-ton skins

Oil for deep frying
Sour cream for topping

To make salsa:

Finely chop tomatillos, tomato, onion and cilantro. Whirl green chilies in food processor or blender until smooth. Mix together tomatillos, tomato, onion, cilantro, green chilies and white wine vinegar. Add salt to taste if desired. Cover and refrigerate 6 hours or overnight.

To make egg roll filling:

Fry chorizo and onion in medium skillet until chorizo is crumbly. Drain well. Add beans, cheese, cumin and cayenne pepper (use more pepper if you like it hotter). Stir until cheese is melted. Let cool to room temperature.

To assemble:

Place 1 teaspoon of filling close to one corner of won-ton wrapper. Fold corner over filling to cover. Fold over left and right corners, then brush sides and top of triangle with water. Roll, sealing corner. Place on a baking sheet and cover while rest of skins are filled.

In a deep pan, pour vegetable oil to depth of 1" and heat to 360°; fry 7 or 8 filled rolls at a time until golden brown, 2 to 3 minutes. Remove and drain on paper towels. Keep warm in a 200° oven until all are done. Serve warm with salsa and sour cream. Makes 24 egg rolls.

Mushroom Delights

Harry E. Wendt

When you're lucky enough to find the BIG mushrooms in your market, think of this dish. It's another one whose simplicity belies its outstanding taste. Those jumbo babies can be stuffed ahead of time and refrigerated, covered with plastic wrap. Heat them just before or after your guests arrive. Harry Wendt brought these to MetroCenter when he was a finalist in the 1988 Easy Entertaining contest.

▼▼▼▼▼▼▼▼▼▼▼▼▼▼▼▼▼▼▼▼▼▼▼

1 pound large mushrooms (2″ to 3″ wide)
1 pound hot Italian bulk sausage
1 small bunch green onions
1 package (8 ounces) cream cheese

Pull stems from mushrooms and discard, or save for another use. In a skillet, cook sausage until done; drain and crumble. Return to pan. Chop green onions. Add green onions to sausage in skillet. Stir in the cream cheese over low heat until cheese melts. (If mixture is too stiff, add a little milk.) Stuff mushroom centers with mixture. Place on cookie sheet. Preheat oven to 350° and heat for 20 minutes, or microwave 4 minutes on high on a microwave-safe pie plate. Makes 20 to 30 mushrooms.

Prickly Pear Jelly

Julie Lawson

This is another Arizona favorite. It's been around at least as long as sugar has been in the state, I'm sure. Some creative pioneer cook just couldn't wait to try making jelly out of those beautiful red prickly pear fruit—once he or she learned from the Indian neighbors that it was good to eat.

This recipe came from Julie Lawson of Mormon Lake. It's in the appetizer section so you can impress your guests (and get out of the kitchen fast) by serving it over a brick of cream cheese with crackers.

An alternate method of juicing the pears came from a Recipe Round Table reader, who advised us to freeze them until they burst, then mash them in a colander with the back of a wooden spoon until the pears yield all their red juice.

▼▼▼▼▼▼▼▼▼▼▼▼▼▼▼▼▼▼▼▼

3 cups prickly pear juice
   (*directions follow*)
1/2 cup lemon juice

1 package pectin
5 cups sugar

Prickly pear juice:

Scrub the spines off prickly pears with a stiff brush (do not peel them). Slice the fruit into ¼" thick pieces. In saucepan, combine 4 cups of the sliced fruit and ½ cup water. Simmer, covered, for 20 minutes, or until soft, mashing the fruit as it cooks. Strain through cheesecloth and discard pulp. Repeat procedure until all fruit is reduced to juice. Let juice stand overnight so that the sediment settles to the bottom. Strain once again before using.

To make jelly, combine juices and pectin. Bring to boil over high heat, stirring constantly. Add sugar; reduce heat to medium, stirring constantly until liquid reaches a rolling boil. Boil hard for 2½ minutes. Remove from heat and skim foam off the top of the liquid. Pour into 12-ounce jars that have been sterilized in boiling water for 20 minutes. Wipe rim of jars and seal with lids. Process in boiling water bath for 5 minutes. Makes 4 12-ounce jars.

Jalapeño Pickled Eggs

Joan Gordon

This is the only recipe in this book from a Chief Justice of the Arizona Supreme Court. Joan Gordon, wife of Frank X. Gordon, was a finalist with this in the 1982 Taste of Arizona contest; it qualifies as a gen-u-ine Arizona favorite. Joan said at the contest that her husband developed this recipe based on the flavor of eggs he ate as a young man in Kingman, where he was raised. He often passed through Grasshopper Junction, north of Kingman on U.S. Highway 93; similar pickled eggs were served with beer in a local bar. This one is warm! Those who do not savor heat can omit the tepins and maybe even the hot yellow chilies. Fire-eaters will love it as printed here. (Prepare this recipe three days before serving.)

▼▼▼▼▼▼▼▼▼▼▼▼▼▼▼▼▼▼▼▼

**3 dozen small eggs, hard-
  cooked and peeled**
1 quart cider vinegar
**1 jar (12 ounces) hot yellow
  chilie peppers packed in
  vinegar, drained**

2 large onions, sliced
3 pickled jalapeño peppers
1/4 cup salt
**6 to 10 red-hot dry chilie
  tepins (optional)**
Boiling water

Put all ingredients in a gallon jar; fill the jar to the top with boiling water. Cover the jar with plastic wrap. Screw on the lid and leave at room temperature. Turn the jar to mix every day. Refrigerate after 5 days. Makes 3 dozen pickled eggs.

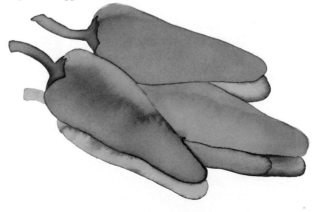

Encore Dip

John Ulmschneider

John Ulmschneider came from Lake Havasu City in 1981, the first of a series of interesting men who were contest finalists. His recipe typifies a certain type of culinary creativity I see in men who came to cooking before it was a yuppie hobby: bold use of ingredients, served in a colorful and generous way. He brought his Encore Dip, centered in a lifesaving ring from his pool. Those who watch their sodium levels can substitute a clove or two of mashed garlic for the garlic salt in this recipe; to cut down even further, rinse the chopped beef with water and pat dry before dicing.

▼▼▼▼▼▼▼▼▼▼▼▼▼▼▼▼▼▼▼▼▼

1 package (3 ounces) cream
  cheese, plain or with
  pimentos
2 cups dairy sour cream
2 teaspoons horseradish
2 teaspoons garlic salt
1 1/2 teaspoons Worcestershire sauce
3 drops Tabasco sauce
1 package (2 1/2 ounces)
  chopped beef, diced
1 cup green olives with
  pimentos, sliced
1/2 cup green bell pepper,
  diced
1/2 cup onion, diced
3 tablespoons yellow banana
  peppers, seeded and diced

Mash softened cream cheese with fork and blend well with sour cream until mixture is smooth. Add horseradish, garlic salt, Worcestershire and Tabasco sauces; blend well. Add remaining ingredients; mix thoroughly. Cover and chill for 2 hours or more to enhance flavors. Keeps well for 3 to 4 days. May be used also as a delicious topping for baked potatoes. Makes 4 cups.

Mexican Christmas Tree Salad

Carol P. Wilson

This is not a salad. What it is is probably THE most popular appetizer in Arizona in the late '70s and the 1980s. Every year we got several versions of this multi-layered dip submitted to the contest. This one won the appetizer category prize in 1986, Festive Favorites, for Carol P. Wilson of Phoenix, who wrote:

"This tasty, colorful appetizer has been a hit for me at teacher luncheons, church potlucks, 'bring a dish' to friends' homes and in-home entertaining. I always take it to all the Christmas functions I attend where a dish is requested, and it has never failed me."

▼▼▼▼▼▼▼▼▼▼▼▼▼▼▼▼▼▼▼▼▼▼

1 pound very lean ground beef
1 package taco seasoning mix
1 can (15 ounces) refried beans
3 avocados, peeled
Juice of 1 lemon
Garlic powder to taste
Dash of salt
1 tablespoon picante sauce
1 carton (8 ounces) sour cream
4 green onions, finely chopped
1 can (4 ounces) chopped black olives
1 can (4 ounces) chopped green chiles
6 ounces Cheddar cheese, grated
6 ounces mozzarella or Monterey Jack cheese, grated
3 tomatoes, chopped
1 head iceberg lettuce, finely shredded
Tortilla chips

In a large skillet over medium to high heat, or an electric skillet set at 350°, brown the meat. Drain off any oil. Add taco seasoning mix and refried beans to the skillet with the meat, stirring it all together thoroughly. Cook the mixture at medium to low heat for about 5 minutes, or until it bubbles. Turn the heat down to low or warm.

In a medium-size bowl, puree avocados with lemon juice. Add garlic powder, dash of salt and picante sauce.

On a large serving platter (12" to 16" round works best), spread warm meat-and-bean base. Top with prepared avocado. Add the rest of the ingredients one at a time in order listed, making each layer a bit smaller in size so that the salad tiers like a Christmas tree. Serve with the tortilla chips. Makes about 25 servings.

Pickled Mushrooms

Lee Scott Theisen

These piquant mushrooms, from the 1981 Movable Feast contest, are perfect picnic or party fare. They will keep a good long time in the refrigerator after you make them, but be forewarned — the minute the mushroom-lover in your family finds these, they're history.

▼▼▼▼▼▼▼▼▼▼▼▼▼▼▼▼▼▼▼

3 cups white wine
4 tablespoons Japanese rice vinegar or cider vinegar
2 stalks celery, coarsely chopped
4 tablespoons olive oil

4 teaspoons salt
2 cloves garlic, peeled and crushed
1 pound fresh mushroom caps, wiped clean with a damp cloth

Clean 2 pint-size canning jars and lids by running them through a dishwasher cycle or by immersing in boiling water.

In a 2-quart saucepan, simmer all ingredients except the mushroom caps for 10 minutes. Strain the liquid and return it to the pan. Add the mushrooms and simmer for 2 to 5 minutes. Pour the mushrooms into the jars and cover with liquid, being careful to screw the lids down tightly. Refrigerate. Makes 2 pints.

Glazed Chicken Strips

Donna Trocono

Scottsdale resident Donna Trocono said she had been making this recipe for years and everyone requested the recipe when she decided to enter it in the 1986 Festive Favorites competition. The presentation is lovely — chicken strips piled in a bread basket, ringed with holly or other seasonal decorations on a platter.

▼▼▼▼▼▼▼▼▼▼▼▼▼▼▼▼▼▼▼

10 to 12 chicken breasts, skinned and boned
1/4 cup flour
1 teaspoon crushed garlic
1/2 teaspoon seasoned salt
1 teaspoon paprika
1/2 teaspoon dried dill

1/2 cup oil
1 cup dry white wine
1 teaspoon dry mustard
1/3 cup wine vinegar
1/3 cup catsup
2 tablespoons brown sugar
Toasted bread basket

Cut each breast into 3 or 4 finger-size strips. Measure flour, garlic, seasoned salt, paprika and dill into plastic bag. Toss chicken strips, a few at a time, in mixture; shake off excess. Brown chicken strips in skillet in heated oil. Do not overcrowd the pan.

Remove to shallow 9″ by 13″ ovenproof dish. Arrange strips in single layer. Blend wine, wine vinegar, brown sugar, catsup and dry mustard. Spoon over chicken. Bake at 375° until tender and glazed, about 20 minutes. Pile into toasted bread basket. Drizzle any remaining sauce over top. Makes 6 to 8 servings.

Toasted bread basket:

Cut the top from a loaf of round, unsliced bread, to make a lid. Remove center of bread and use for another purpose. Brush inside and lid with melted butter, flavored if you wish with favorite seasonings or herbs. Toast at 375° degrees until hot and crisp, 10 to 15 minutes.

Love Those Spiced Walnuts

Rebecca Keck

Who doesn't love an easy, fast microwave recipe? This one comes from Rebecca Keck, who was a category winner in 1986 and a finalist again in 1988. She lived in Clarkdale in 1986, but had a Phoenix address for her second appearance, this time at the MetroCenter cook-off (*Holiday tip:* Double, triple or quadruple the cinnamon, allspice, nutmeg and clove amounts to make fresh pumpkin pie spice for baking. To grind whole spices, use an electric coffee or spice mill. Clean it by grinding white rice.)

▼▼▼▼▼▼▼▼▼▼▼▼▼▼▼▼▼▼▼▼▼▼▼

1/2 cup packed brown sugar
1/2 teaspoon salt
1 teaspoon pumpkin pie
 spice, *or* 1/2 teaspoon
 cinnamon

1/4 teaspoon allspice
1/8 teaspoon nutmeg
1/8 teaspoon cloves
1 1/2 tablespoons water
1 1/2 cups walnut halves

Combine all ingredients except the walnuts in a 2-quart, microwave-safe bowl. Microwave on high for 3 minutes, stirring occasionally. Stir in the walnuts, ½-cup at a time, until well-coated. Microwave on high for 5 minutes, or until syrup hardens slightly. Spoon onto waxed paper to cool. Makes 6 to 8 servings.

Cheese Nut Ball

Agatha Pavsner

Would holiday entertaining exist if the cheese-nut ball had not been invented? I doubt it. It has many virtues—first of all, it is simple to make. You only have to be able to mix things to make a cheese ball. It can be made well in advance and tucked away in the refrigerator until company, planned or unplanned, shows up on the doorstep. Like an omelette, it takes well to many additions, using up a bit of this and a leftover of that—whatever may be hanging around in the 'fridge. Plus, it is appropriate for almost all occasions, so you can take it anywhere, fan out an array of crackers and impress your hostess or your guests with your culinary skill. Agatha Pavsner from Sun City proved this recipe's portability when she was a 1981 finalist in The Movable Feast contest.

▼▼▼▼▼▼▼▼▼▼▼▼▼▼▼▼▼▼▼▼

1 package (8 ounces) cream cheese
1 jar (5 ounces) sharp Cheddar cheese spread
1/4 cup crumbled Roquefort cheese
3 tablespoons milk or cream
1 teaspoon grated onion
1 teaspoon Worcestershire sauce
2/3 cup chopped pecans or peanuts
1/3 cup finely chopped parsley

Combine cheeses in a large bowl, cover and let warm to room temperature. Add milk or cream, onion and Worcestershire sauce. Beat slowly until well-mixed. Line a small (1 pint) bowl with a sheet of plastic wrap, leaving 3″ to 4″ hanging over rim of bowl. Spoon mixture into bowl. Gather edges of wrap up tightly over cheese to make a ball. Tie ends securely. Chill overnight.

When ready to serve, remove plastic wrap carefully and shape cheese into two smooth balls or logs, about one cup each. Combine nuts and parsley in a pie-pan or medium-size bowl. Roll ball in mixture until covered. Serve with assortment of crackers. Makes 2 (10 ounces each) 5½″ balls or logs.

Honeydew Lemonade

Bettie Brown

Casa Grande resident Bettie Brown is a native Arizonan, raised on a cattle ranch near Globe. She loves to cook and was a *Republic* cook-off finalist for the second time in 1988 when she brought this to the Easy Entertaining contest for our beverages category. The judges thought it was a perfect summer cooler.

▼▼▼▼▼▼▼▼▼▼▼▼▼▼▼▼▼▼▼

Rind of 2 lemons, removed in strips with a vegetable peeler
1 cup fresh lemon juice
3/4 cup sugar
1 honeydew melon (about 3 1/2 pounds), seed and rind removed, cut into 1″ cubes (about 6 cups)

2 cups cold water
2 cups ice cubes
GARNISH:
Thin lemon slices
Mint leaves

In a small saucepan, combine the lemon rind, lemon juice and sugar. Bring the mixture to a boil over medium heat, stirring until the sugar is dissolved. Boil for about 5 minutes. Pour the syrup through a sieve set over a bowl and let cool.

In a food processor, puree the honeydew. Force puree through a fine seive set over a bowl. In an attractive pitcher, combine syrup, puree and 2 cups of cold water. Stir well.

Just before time to serve, stir in 2 cups of ice cubes and garnish the lemonade with the lemon slices and mint sprigs. Makes about 8 cups.

Oyster Patties

Dedra Cannon

In the 1986 Festive Favorites contest, Dedra Cannon of Phoenix wrote that this recipe has been in her family for at least seventy years. It came from New Orleans and was always made by her mother and grandmother for Thanksgiving and Christmas. "We also serve them as a side dish with the meal when they're not served as an appetizer," Cannon wrote. "They're delicious with a chilled glass of white wine."

▼▼▼▼▼▼▼▼▼▼▼▼▼▼▼▼▼▼▼▼▼

4 boxes Pepperidge Farm pastry shells (six shells per box)

2 dozen Louisiana oysters, with oyster liquid

4 stalks celery, minced

2 cloves garlic, minced

1 bunch green onions, minced

1/3 bunch parsley, minced

2 tablespoons butter

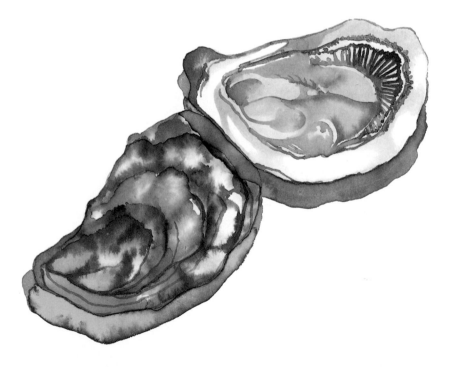

Bake pastry shells according to directions on the box. Let cool, then remove pastry from inside the shells with a fork. Put aside in a bowl for later use.

Melt butter in skillet or large saucepan. Sauté celery until slightly soft, then add green onions. Sauté for about 3 minutes then add garlic, stirring constantly.

After mixture becomes soft, add the insides of the patty shells and water from the oysters. Consistency should be like a thick gravy. If necessary, add water to keep the mixture from becoming too thick.

Once the pastry mixture cooks down, add the oysters and cook until the butter rises to the top, about 10 to 15 minutes. Oysters will shrink when cooked. Add the parsley, and stir for about 1 minute. Fill each patty shell with at least one oyster and some of the mixture. Put pastry top on to cover.

The patty shells can be filled and refrigerated, then warmed in the oven at 300° when ready to serve. Makes 2 dozen.

Hot Chocolate on Ice

Barbara Gilbert

Barbara Gilbert is a marvelous cook, which was evident to anybody reading the numerous contributions she submitted to the *Republic's* Recipe Round Table column in the Food section. This recipe brought her from Sun City to MetroCenter for the 1988 Easy Entertaining finals. Barbara was also a finalist in 1983, in the Just Desserts competition.

▼▼▼▼▼▼▼▼▼▼▼▼▼▼▼▼▼▼▼▼▼

1/4 cup unsweetened cocoa
1/4 cup sugar
3 cups milk

1/8 teaspoon salt (optional)
1 teaspoon vanilla

In saucepan, stir cocoa, sugar, milk and salt, if desired, over moderate heat until sugar is dissolved. Add vanilla. Pour into an 8" by 8" metal pan and freeze.

Before serving, remove from freezer and let stand 20 minutes. Break up and stir with an electric mixer until thick and creamy and full of ice crystals. Serve in chilled glasses. Makes 4 servings.

SOUPS AND SALADS

This section, Soups and Salads, contains some of
the most satisfying and versatile kinds of dishes.
They can be side dishes, served before an entree
to round out a menu. Some of them, such as
Vietnamese Chicken Salad with Hot Tahini
Sauce and Shrimp Jicama Salad with Piquant
Tequila Dressing, are excellent, well-rounded
meals by themselves.

Several soups here have a Mexican accent—
Caldo Xochitl, Caldo de Queso y Chili Verde, for
example. A couple more are Southwestern inventions, such as the grand-prize-winning Sweet
Potato Jalapeno Soup with Lime Cream.

What's so intriguing about the Mexican soups
is that most of the recipes are for dishes seldom
seen on restaurant menus. A couple—Sopa de
Albondigas and Tortilla Soup—are timeless
Arizona favorites, even though the recipes aren't
exactly standards in *Joy of Cooking*.

The salad selections are creative inventions
from the contest files, stretching well beyond
lettuce-tomato-carrot combos. In fact, there are
a few that can even be served to people who
don't like lettuce. For those folks, serve Self-
Dressing Salad, Salad Skewers, or Sunflower-
Walnut Salad.

Sopa De Albondigas (Meatball soup)

Donna Eckert

Mint leaves are the authentic touch in Sopa de Albondigas, the popular Mexican meatball soup, submitted by Donna Eckert of Phoenix in the 1982 Taste of Arizona recipe contest. Eckert specified that the meatballs should be 1″ in diameter. Albondigas fans who seek it out in the state's restaurants know that meatball size is a cook's personal statement. You can find them in all sizes, from as small as marbles to as large as billiard balls.

▼▼▼▼▼▼▼▼▼▼▼▼▼▼▼▼▼▼▼

BROTH:
2 tablespoons oil
1 medium onion, sliced
4 cups water
1 can (16 ounces) tomato chunks with juice
1 tablespoon fresh cilantro, chopped
8 dried mint leaves
1 teaspoon dried oregano
3 whole canned green chilies, chopped

1 small bunch green onions, including tops, sliced
1 teaspoon salt
MEATBALLS:
1 pound extra-lean ground beef
1 egg
1 teaspoon dried oregano
3 mint leaves, dried and crushed
1/4 cup minced onion
OPTIONAL:
Cooked rice (*See note below*).

To make soup:

In large saucepan, heat oil and lightly sauté medium sliced onion. Add water, tomato chunks with juice, cilantro, mint leaves, oregano, green chilies, green onions and salt. Bring to a boil and simmer, covered, for 10 minutes.

While soup is simmering, combine ground beef, egg, oregano, mint leaves and minced onion. Mix well. Form into 1″ balls and drop into boiling broth. Boil, covered, over low heat for 30 minutes. Makes 6 to 8 servings

Note: You may add cooked, well-rinsed rice to meatballs or broth; be sure to rinse the rice well, however; otherwise it will cloud the broth.

Caldo De Queso Y Chili Verde
(Cheese and Green Chili Soup)

Ledean Vacovsky

Like many soups, this one is better served the next day, noted Ledean Vacovsky of Tucson when she submitted this recipe to the Zest of the Southwest contest. In other words, here's another candidate perfect for entertaining.

Roasting fresh green chilies is one of the basic techniques of Southwestern cooking. Ledean's original instructions called for placing the roasted chilies in the freezer for three hours after they are charred. This works, but if you are pressed for time, you can also place them in a paper bag for about 20 minutes, with the top rolled down. The moisture of the chilies will steam off the skin as they cool in the bag.

Chilies can also be roasted on a barbecue grill, turning with tongs as they blacken. The trick to peeling them is to be sure that they are charred but not burned all over, so the green meat just under the skin is roasted throughout. Many cooks do not use any oil to roast their peppers.

A lot of people consider that roasted-green-chilie taste to be one of the definitive flavors of our cuisine.

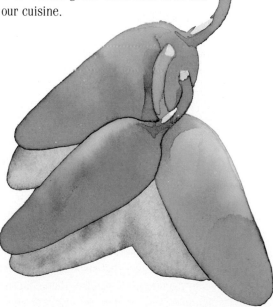

▼▼▼▼▼▼▼▼▼▼▼▼▼▼▼▼▼▼▼▼

2 tablespoons butter
2 onions, diced
4 cloves fresh garlic, chopped
1 large can (28 ounces) roasted diced green chilies or 15 freshly roasted green chilies, diced (*chilie-roasting instructions below*)

5 ripe tomatoes, diced
6 medium white potatoes, peeled and cut into 1" cubes
16 cups water
2 pounds Longhorn Colby or Cheddar cheese, shredded
Salt to taste

In a large soup pot, melt butter and sauté onions and garlic over medium heat. When onions are soft, add green chilies and tomatoes. Simmer 10 minutes, stirring every minute or so. Add potatoes and water. Cook over medium heat until potatoes are done, 10 to 20 minutes. Add cheese and, on very low heat, simmer about 30 minutes. Add salt to taste. For best results, allow to cool overnight and serve the next day. Makes 6 servings.

To roast chilies:

Fresh green chilies
Olive oil

Dip each chilie in olive oil and place on cookie sheet. Place under broiler, about 3" from heat source. Broil until chilies are slightly scorched. Turn chilies and repeat process. It will take only 3 to 4 minutes on each side. Place chilies in freezer 3 hours. Remove and pull skin from flesh of chilies. Remove seeds and membranes. Use with any recipe calling for green chilies.

Mamacita's Mexican Soup

Becca Gardner

This is another Zest of the Southwest recipe, from Phoenix resident Becca Gardner. If making stock sounds like too much trouble on first glance, please just read through the rest of the recipe. You can throw all the stock ingredients together one evening, let it simmer while you do something else, then chill the strained broth until you plan to serve it, preferably within two days.

To make this even more substantial, you can put a half-cup of rice in each bowl before pouring in the soup.

▼▼▼▼▼▼▼▼▼▼▼▼▼▼▼▼▼▼▼▼

STOCK:
2 1/2 quarts water
5 cloves garlic
3 fresh oregano sprigs
2 whole cloves
1 tablespoon salt
1 tablespoon ground cumin
1 teaspoon black pepper
3 bay leaves, broken
1 or 2 fresh basil sprigs
   (1 teaspoon dried basil if
   fresh is not available)
5 chicken bouillon cubes
1 frying chicken (3 pounds)
   cut up

VEGETABLES:
Juice of two limes
1 medium zucchini, chopped
1 yellow onion, chopped
2 stalks celery, chopped
1 carrot, chopped
1 green bell pepper, seeded
   and chopped
1 can (17 ounces) garbanzo
   beans, drained
OPTIONAL GARNISHES:
Cooked rice
Sliced avocados
Fresh salsa

To make stock:

Bring the water to a boil, and then add all the stock ingredients, including the chicken. Skim the foam from the top as the soup simmers for 1 to 1½ hours. Remove the chicken, debone it and shred the meat when cool. Strain the stock and chill. This hardens the fat for easy removal.

To make soup:

Remove fat from stock. Reheat and add the juice of two limes. Add all the vegetables except the beans and cook just until tender-crisp, about 20 minutes. Add the shredded chicken and garbanzo beans. Heat until chicken and beans are hot throughout.

To serve the soup, ladle into large soup bowls (over one-half cup rice if desired). Garnish with sliced avocados and fresh salsa. Makes 8 servings.

Blender Gazpacho

Janet Smith

In 1981, Janet Smith of Tempe submitted this popular favorite to the Movable Feast contest, which asked for recipes suitable for picnics. This version is made in the blender or food processor. In my opinion, olive oil and wine vinegar are the perfect counterpoint to gazpacho vegetables.

▼▼▼▼▼▼▼▼▼▼▼▼▼▼▼▼▼▼▼▼▼

**1 can (48 ounces) tomato
  juice
1 small clove garlic
1 medium onion, quartered
1 medium green pepper,
  quartered
2 small or 1 large cucumber,
  unpeeled**

**1 teaspoon salt
1/4 teaspoon pepper
3 tablespoons salad oil
  (preferably olive oil)
3 tablespoons wine or wine
  vinegar**

To make in blender:

Pour one-third tomato juice into blender container. Add onion, garlic, salt and pepper. Blend until vegetables are grated.

Pour mixture into large (3-quart) bowl. Add one-third tomato juice and green pepper and blend until grated. Add this to mixture in bowl. Pour remaining one-third of tomato juice into blender container. Add cucumber, oil and vinegar. Repeat the process. Pour into bowl. Stir mixture to blend. If a finer gazpacho is desired, return some of the mixture to blender and repeat process until the desired texture is reached.

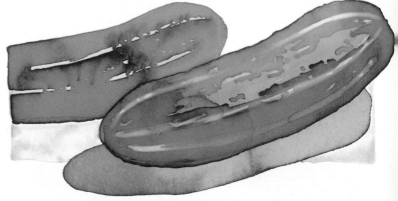

To make in food processor:

Place onion, garlic and green pepper in processor bowl and pulse in short bursts until vegetables are grated. Remove to separate bowl large enough to hold all the soup. Quarter cucumber and pulse processor about 2 seconds, or chop by hand. Add to other vegetables, then stir in the tomato juice, salt, pepper, oil and wine or wine vinegar.

Gazpacho should be made 24 hours ahead of time and refrigerated so flavors blend and develop. Serves 8 to 10.

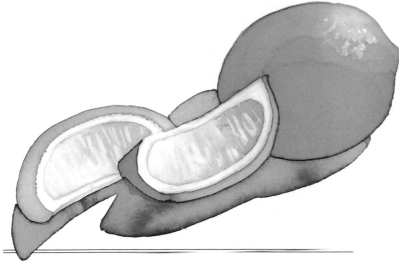

Sweet Potato Jalapeño Soup with Lime Cream

Carolyn M. Ness

This simple yet beautifully sophisticated soup wowed the judges at the 1988 Easy Entertaining contest, and was awarded the $1,000 grand prize. Creator Carolyn Ness of Gilbert immediately called home and told her father, to whom she had served the soup countless times as she refined it.

Before moving to Arizona, Ness worked at a winery in California, and ate at many restaurants in San Francisco, Napa and Sonoma. Somewhere along the way, she said, she had a sweet potato soup. After she moved to Arizona, she decided it needed a bit more pizazz—thus the jalapeños. That's how grand prize winners are born.

▼▼▼▼▼▼▼▼▼▼▼▼▼▼▼▼▼▼▼▼▼

SOUP:
4 medium sweet potatoes
  or yams
Salted water to cover
  potatoes
1 cup diced red onion
2 tablespoons unsalted
  butter

4 cups chicken stock
2 fresh jalapeño peppers,
  seeded and finely diced
Salt and pepper to taste
4 sprigs cilantro
LIME CREAM:
2 limes
1/2 cup sour cream

To prepare soup:

Cook sweet potatoes whole and unpeeled, covered, in salted water, about 1 hour. Drain, cool and peel.

To prepare lime cream:

Stir the juice and grated peel of 2 limes into sour cream to attain a pourable consistency. Refrigerate until ready to use.

Finish soup:

In small skillet, sauté onion in butter until soft. Puree potatoes, onion and 1 cup stock in blender or food processor. Place in a saucepan. Add remaining stock, jalapeños, salt and pepper. Cover and simmer over low heat for about 30 minutes.

Stir the soup and ladle into bowls. Swirl a spoonful of the lime cream into each bowl. Garnish with cilantro. Makes 4 servings.

Caldo Xochitl (Pretty Soup)

Stephanie Goble

The name of this dish is Aztec for "Pretty Soup" (that weird-looking word is pronounced SO-cheel). And is it ever pretty. It's perfect for buffet entertaining, since all the ingredients should be at room temperature before serving. Boiling broth is poured over them just before serving.

Glendale resident Stephanie Goble won in the "starters" category with this recipe in the 1987 Zest of the Southwest contest. She collected the recipe from the Hotel Aranzazu in Guadalajara, Mexico.

▼▼▼▼▼▼▼▼▼▼▼▼▼▼▼▼▼▼▼▼▼

1/2 broiler/fryer chicken
2 cloves garlic
1/4 bunch cilantro
1/2 teaspoon whole black
  peppercorns
2 quarts water

3 fresh Serrano chilies
3 limes
1 medium carrot
1 1/2 cups cooked white rice
1 large or 2 small tomatoes
1 avocado

All the vegetables and the rice should be at room temperature. The boiling broth will heat them to serving temperature. Quantities of vegetables can be adjusted to suit your taste. If you don't like one of the ingredients, leave it out.

Simmer chicken, garlic, 2 sprigs cilantro and the peppercorns, covered, in 2 quarts water for 1 hour. Remove chicken, let cool and remove meat from the bones. Shred and set aside. Skim and discard the fat from the broth, along with the garlic, peppercorns and cilantro. Leave broth in the pan.

Wearing rubber gloves, slice the Serrano chilies lengthwise. Scrape out seeds with the tip of a teaspoon and discard. Remove the stems and chop the chilies finely. Set aside in a small serving bowl.

Cut the limes into quarters and set aside on a small serving plate. Peel the carrot and slice into very thin rounds. Add to the chicken broth. Reheat the chicken broth over high heat while you prepare the rest of the soup.

Divide the rice among 6 heat-proof soup bowls. Divide the shredded chicken among the bowls. As you prepare the following ingredients, divide them among the bowls as well.

Finely chop the green onions, including part of the green stems. Finely chop the remaining cilantro leaves. Cut the tomatoes in half crossways, squeeze out the seeds, remove the stem and chop coarsely. Peel and cut the avocado into 6 slices.

The broth should be at a full, rolling boil. Divide the boiling broth among the bowls. Serve immediately with the limes and chilies on the side. Squeeze lime juice into the soup and add as many chilies as you like. Makes 6 servings.

Tortilla Soup

Phyllis Cooper

This delicious dish originated when Mexican households needed to use up leftover corn tortillas, which become a sort of crouton in the finished product. A faster way to crisp tortilla chips is to dip the strips of tortillas in oil and then crisp them in the oven. Phyllis Cooper of Phoenix submitted this recipe to the Zest of the Southwest contest in 1987.

The supplement published in the November 8 *Republic* was one of the most popular recipe tabloids we ever printed. Dozens of readers asked for extra copies to send to out-of-state relatives.

▼▼▼▼▼▼▼▼▼▼▼▼▼▼▼▼▼▼▼▼

1/2 cup oil
6 small corn tortillas, cut
 into 1" strips
1 yellow onion, chopped
1 clove garlic, chopped
1 can (8 ounces) tomato
 sauce

1/2 teaspoon cumin
6 cups rich chicken stock
1/2 cup grated Monterey
 Jack cheese
1 large ripe tomato, finely
 chopped

In a stockpot, heat oil and fry tortilla strips until crisp. Drain and reserve.

In the same pot and in half of the remaining oil, over medium heat, fry onion and garlic for 3 minutes. Add tomato sauce and cumin and simmer gently for 5 minutes. Pour in chicken stock, simmer for 5 minutes.

Remove from heat. To serve, pour soup over tortilla strips and garnish with grated cheese and chopped tomato.

Makes 6 servings.

Shrimp Jicama Salad with Piquant Tequila Dressing

Virginia L. Yates

Creative cook Virginia L. Yates of Paradise Valley developed this recipe especially for the 1987 Zest of the Southwest cookoff. Her goal: "I wanted to create something that reflected today's Southwest spirit." She succeeded beautifully. Check out the citrus zest in the dressing, and the ingredients of this main-dish salad, perfect for a buffet or impressive pot-luck contribution.

Jicama is the crisp white vegetable that grows like a potato in Mexico. Slightly sweet sticks of jicama (pronounced HIC-ama) are a wonderful addition to a plate of raw vegetables, or serve them along with little dishes of salt and chili powder for dipping.

▼▼▼▼▼▼▼▼▼▼▼▼▼▼▼▼▼▼▼▼▼

DRESSING:
1/2 cup mayonnaise
2 1/2 tablespoons fresh
    lemon juice
1 tablespoon white wine
    Worcestershire sauce
1/2 teaspoon dill weed
1/2 teaspoon cayenne pepper
1/4 teaspoon dry mustard
Juice of 1/2 lime
1/2 teaspoon lemon zest
3/4 teaspoon lime zest

1 cup sour cream
1/2 teaspoon tequila
SALAD:
3 heads butter lettuce
1 1/2 pounds bay (salad)
    shrimp, 60 to 80 to the
    pound
1 medium jicama, in julienne
    strips
2 large avocados, peeled and
    sliced
2 large tomato wedges for
    garnish

To make dressing:

Whisk together mayonnaise, lemon juice, white wine Worcestershire sauce, dill weed, cayenne pepper, dry mustard, lime juice, lemon zest and lime zest. When ingredients are well emulsified, mix in sour cream and add tequila. Refrigerate for 3 hours.

Just before serving:

Tear lettuce into pieces and line a large platter or salad bowl. Top with shrimp, jicama and avocado. Add dressing. Garnish with tomato wedges. Makes 6 servings.

Mexican Salad Supreme

Constance Gagnon

Mexican Salad Supreme takes the ever-popular Taco Salad to new heights. The chili con queso layer adds a separate dimension not usually found in this dish. (Just by itself, the chili con queso is a fine dip for tortilla chips.) Half the fun of this dish is that guests get to layer their own combo. If somebody dislikes black olives, they just skip them.

Mesa resident Constance Gagnon was a finalist in 1982 in the Neuvo Arizona category of the Taste of Arizona contest. She noted that you can vary amounts of all the salad ingredients, depending on how many people you intend to serve.

▼▼▼▼▼▼▼▼▼▼▼▼▼▼▼▼▼▼▼▼

BEEF MIXTURE:
2 1/2 pounds lean ground beef
1 cup onion, chopped
1 cup celery, chopped
1 cup green pepper, chopped
3 cloves garlic
2 to 3 tablespoons chili powder
1 teaspoon salt
1 tablespoon crushed hot red peppers

CHILI CON QUESO:
1 can (16 ounces) tomatoes
1 can (3 1/2 or 4 ounces) chopped green chilies
2 green onions, chopped
2 tablespoons chili powder
Dash of liquid chili pepper sauce (such as Tabasco)
2 pounds pasteurized processed cheese, cut up

SALAD AND TOPPING INGREDIENTS:
1 head of lettuce, chopped
3 large tomatoes, chopped
Tortilla chips
1 cup sour cream
1 1/2 cups guacamole
1 1/2 cups salsa
1 cup black olives, sliced

To make beef mixture:

Brown meat in large skillet over medium heat. Drain well. Add onion, celery, green pepper, garlic, chili powder, salt and crushed red peppers. Simmer 30 minutes. Keep warm.

To make chili con queso:

Combine tomatoes, green chilies, green onions, chili powder and liquid pepper sauce in large saucepan. Simmer 20 minutes. Slowly add cheese, stirring, until melted. Keep warm.

To serve:

Arrange all salad ingredients separately so guests can layer their own salads. Put beef and cheese mixtures and toppings in separate bowls.

Layer in this order: Shredded lettuce, tomatoes, beef mixture, tortilla chips, chili con queso, sour cream, guacamole, black olives, salsa. Makes 8 to 10 servings.

Sunflower Waldorf Salad

Bettie Brown

This modern take on an old favorite was Bettie Brown's winning contribution to our 1984 Healthy Appetites contest. (The Casa Grande resident was a finalist again in 1988.) Yogurt substitutes for the mayonnaise or creamy cooked dressings found on more traditional Waldorfs, and the sunflower seeds add a new kind of crunch.

Although the acid in the yogurt will help keep the banana from browning, it's still best to fold in the bananas shortly before serving.

▼▼▼▼▼▼▼▼▼▼▼▼▼▼▼▼▼▼▼▼▼

2 medium apples, cored and chopped (about 1 1/2 cups)
1/2 cup seedless green grapes, halved
1/2 cup chopped celery
1/2 cup sunflower seeds (unsalted)
1/3 cup plain yogurt
1 large banana, sliced
Lettuce leaves

In a mixing bowl, toss together apples, grapes, celery and sunflower seeds. Fold in yogurt and sliced banana. Serve on individual lettuce-lined salad plates. Garnish with additional banana slices and whole grapes. Makes 4 servings.

Self-Dressing Salad

Katherine Dugan

Every now and then, you run into somebody who says, "I hate salad." Probe a little, and you may find that the REAL objection is not to salad—it's lettuce that's causing the negative opinion. Give these people a tasty raw vegetable combination like this one, and they're perfectly happy. Just don't tell them they're really eating salad. Katherine Dugan sent us this one in 1984, when Healthy Appetites was our contest theme.

▼▼▼▼▼▼▼▼▼▼▼▼▼▼▼▼▼▼▼▼▼▼

1 medium cucumber	**2 cloves garlic**
2 medium tomatoes	**1 teaspoon lemon juice**
2 avocados	**1 teaspoon black pepper**

Peel cucumber and avocados. Core tomatoes. Press or mince garlic. Chop all vegetables into 1" cubes. Mix vegetables, lemon juice, pepper and garlic in bowl. Refrigerate, covered, 1 hour before serving. Makes 4 servings.

Vietnamese Chicken Salad with Hot Tahini Sauce

Paul Michael Suino

Paul Michael Suino of Scottsdale took home $250 as the buffet category winner in the 1988 Easy Entertaining contest for one of the most exotic and tasty chicken salads you will ever find. He got the recipe from a friend who was a Vietnam veteran, and at contest time, presented the judges with an absolutely gorgeous dish. He lined a long oblong bowl with a banana leaf, artfully piled in the salad, and garnished the whole with an orchid—which he made sure was edible!

The dressing is a wonderfully spicy concoction, and it's served on the side so diners can adjust the heat level to personal preference. Tahini is a sesame seed paste which, like Chinese hot oil, can be found in Oriental markets or in supermarket specialty sections.

▼▼▼▼▼▼▼▼▼▼▼▼▼▼▼▼▼▼▼▼

2 whole chicken breasts, skin removed
6 to 10 green onions
1 small carrot
4 to 6 cups shredded bok choy
2 to 3 tablespoons peanuts
DRESSING:
1 tablespoon cold brewed tea

1/4 cup tahini
1 to 2 tablespoons Chinese hot oil
3 tablespoons soy sauce
1/4 cup peanut oil
3 tablespoons red wine vinegar
2 teaspoons sugar
1 clove garlic, minced

Cook the chicken. Cool and cut into thin strips. Cut onions and carrot into thin strips. Mix chicken, onions, carrot and bok choy. Sprinkle peanuts on top.

For the dressing, beat tea into tahini in a small bowl, then mix in all the remaining dressing ingredients.

Serve salad with dressing on the side. Dressing is very spicy, so diners should add it to taste. Makes 6 servings.

Salad Skewers

Barbara Fenzl

Here's another lettuce-less salad. This one was submitted by Barbara Fenzl of Phoenix in our very first cooking contest in 1981, perfect for our make-ahead Movable Feast theme. Today, Barb is active in the Phoenix food scene as the owner of Les Gourmettes Cooking School, food editor of *Phoenix Home and Garden* magazine and energetic leader of numerous projects. She's also well known for her fabulous desserts.

▼▼▼▼▼▼▼▼▼▼▼▼▼▼▼▼▼▼

1 box cherry tomatoes	**MARINADE:**
1/2 pound fresh mushrooms	**2/3 cup oil**
1/2 head cauliflower, broken	**1/2 cup dry white wine**
into flowerets	**3 tablespoons lemon juice**
2 green peppers, cut into	**1/2 teaspoon salt**
squares	**1 clove garlic, crushed**
1 cup ripe olives	**1/4 teaspoon pepper**

Put vegetables in container with tight-fitting lid. In a 2-cup liquid measuring cup or a small mixing bowl, combine oil, wine, lemon juice, salt, garlic and pepper; pour over vegetables. Marinate until serving time. For each serving, place assorted marinated vegetables on wooden skewers. Makes 6 servings.

BREADS

This breads category contains some unusual treats. Here you will find quick breads, sweet breads, yeast breads, even a sourdough bread called Sinkers. Those among us who love quick and easy recipes will enjoy Pumpkin Corn Bread, Fiesta Bread, Mango Bread and Peanut Butter Bread. Yeast-bread devoteés will want to try Soya-Seed Rolls, Southwest Dinner Rolls and Bolillos—Mexico's delicious answer to the French hard roll.

Sourdough bread was one of the most asked-for recipes in Recipe Round Table, the readers' exchange column that ran during the years I was food editor at the *Republic*. In fact, so many people asked about it that I finally wrote a long feature story on the subject, and unearthed dozens of recipes as well as a lot of history. Sourdough has to be coddled in the summer in Phoenix, but with refrigeration, the starter can survive.

I think this chapter reflects some of the most specialized experiments of our contestants. Baking success depends on certain unalterable principles, and tinkering with ingredients requires a certain level of skill. Through the years I have learned that baking success or failure depends most of all on proper oven temperature. Unfortunately, many (if not most) ovens are calibrated incorrectly. The easiest way to correct the problem is to buy an oven thermometer and use it, adjusting the temperature upwards 25° if the dial says 350° but the thermometer inside says 325°.

Sinkers (Sourdough Biscuits)

Ernie Startup

When Phoenix resident Ernie Startup was a finalist in the 1982 Taste of Arizona contest, she made sourdough biscuits. She had had her starter since 1965, and the Colorado woman who gave it to her said it had been alive since 1911. This recipe was Ernie's update of an old-fashioned family favorite. She said at the time: "My mother, a schoolmarm-turned-ranch wife, was famous for her yeast biscuits and made them in a Dutch oven. I add dry yeast and make them in an electric skillet." Making them also made her feel connected to her father, who grew wheat in Texas in the early part of this century.

Sourdough has a long and colorful pioneer history. Gold miners in Alaska made it famous—they would even take their precious starter to bed with them to keep it warm through the nights. Research indicates that the primitive practice of keeping a piece of fermented dough, ready to start the next batch for baking, goes back a long, long way in history. With modern yeast, it's easier than ever to tame the elusive sour beast. Ernie's recipe is a model of direction.

▼▼▼▼▼▼▼▼▼▼▼▼▼▼▼▼▼▼▼▼

1 tablespoon dry yeast
2 cups cool water
1 teaspoon honey
1/2 cup non-fat dry milk
2 tablespoons brown sugar
2 teaspoons salt
1 1/2 cups sourdough
  starter (*made in advance;*
  recipe follows)

1/2 cup rolled oats
1 cup whole wheat flour
1/2 cup sunflower seeds
4 1/2 to 5 cups bread flour
1 tablespoon corn oil
Cornmeal

Put dry yeast in large glass crockery or plastic bowl. Do *not* use metal bowl. Pour cool water—it should be no warmer than 80°—over yeast and mix to dissolve. Add honey and let sit a couple of minutes. Then add non-fat dry milk, sugar, salt, sourdough starter, oats, whole wheat flour and sunflower seeds. Mix thoroughly.

Add enough bread flour to make a sticky dough. The amount of flour will depend on how thick the sourdough was.

Turn out on lightly floured board and let rest while you scrape
all the dough from the bowl. Without washing the bowl, grease it with
corn oil. Knead for about 10 minutes, until the dough is nice and
bouncy but not too firm. Return dough to greased bowl and make a
seal by dipping your fingers in water and running them around the
top of the bowl; then cover with plastic wrap. Put the covered bowl
in a draft-free place where air temperature is not more than 80°;
let dough rise for at least 1 hour. If the room is cool, it won't hurt
to let dough sit for 1½ hours.

Turn out on lightly floured board and divide into 36 pieces. Roll
each piece into a ball and dip one side first in corn oil and then in
cornmeal. Place the pieces on a cookie sheet with cornmeal side
down and far enough apart so that they can rise without touching.
Cover and put in a place where the temperature is about 90° to rise.

When they double in size, about 1 hour later, heat electric skillet
to 180° and carefully remove enough biscuits from the cookie sheet
to fill the skillet. Put the lid on and don't peek for 5 minutes. They
should be nicely browned on the down side. Turn the biscuits over
and put the lid back; bake an additional 5 minutes.

Remove to wire rack and repeat process. Cool biscuits on the
wire rack before toasting and buttering. Because they have no
shortening, they are rather firm, with large holes to hold lots of butter and Arizona sour orange marmalade.

Sourdough starter:

Place 1 cup milk in a glass jar or crock and let stand at room
temperature 24 hours. Stir in 1 cup flour and leave uncovered in a
warm place 2 to 5 days, until it starts to bubble. It is ready to use.
Between uses, stir in more flour and milk and set aside overnight
before refrigerating.

Soya Seed Rolls

Gwen Gurule

Since so many people have allergies these days, you might find yourself entertaining someone who has special needs. That's exactly the position in which Gwen Gurule of Sun City found herself. Here is what she wrote when she submitted this in the 1986 Festive Favorites cookoff, "I first made these rolls to accommodate a holiday guest with a wheat allergy. Everyone was quite taken with them. Everyone thinks they're made with a regular wheat flour and some 'secret' ingredient. They've become an established favorite with everyone, especially with Uncle Ed, who loves bread and hates soybeans! The rolls are a nice break from heavy, filling breads and have an obvious nutritional bonus."

▼▼▼▼▼▼▼▼▼▼▼▼▼▼▼▼▼▼▼▼▼

2 tablespoons yeast	6 1/2 cups soy flour
1 1/2 cups lukewarm water	1 teaspoon salt
1/4 cup oil	1/3 cup poppy seeds
1/2 cup honey	

Dissolve yeast in water. Add oil and honey. Mix dry ingredients in separate container. Combine all ingredients and mix well. Knead 15 minutes. Let rise in oiled bowl in warm place for 60 minutes. Knead again briefly. Shape into rolls. Place on oiled baking sheet, cover lightly with towel and let rise for 30 minutes. Twenty minutes before baking, preheat oven to 350°. Bake at 350 for 20 to 25 minutes. Makes 12 rolls.

Arizona Margarita Bread

Harold Freeman

Phoenix optometrist Harold Freeman adapted his mother's recipe,
substituting dates and tequila for prunes and brandy, to create Arizona Margarita Bread for the Taste of Arizona contest in 1982. He
won in the Western category, our first male prize winner. (The
judges said afterwards that he nearly took the grand prize.) When
you make this dessert bread, do try the flavored cream cheese
spread that Harold served with his tasty concoction.

▼▼▼▼▼▼▼▼▼▼▼▼▼▼▼▼▼▼▼▼

1 cup pitted dates, chopped
1/4 cup tequila
1/4 cup orange-flavored
  liqueur
1/2 cup warm water
1 teaspoon each grated
  lemon and lime peel
2/3 cup brown sugar, firmly
  packed

2 tablespoons shortening
1 large egg
2 cups sifted all-purpose
  flour
1 teaspoon baking soda
1 teaspoon salt
2/3 cup chopped pecans
Cheese spread (*recipe*
  ***follows*)**

Preheat oven to 350°. In small bowl, combine dates, tequila, liqueur,
water, lemon and lime peel; set aside. In large mixing bowl, using
an electric mixer, beat sugar, shortening and egg until fluffy. In another bowl, combine flour, soda and salt. Add to creamed mixture
alternately with date mixture, using low to medium speed. Stir in
pecans. Turn into greased 9" by 5" by 2 ½" inch loaf pan. Bake at 350°
for 50 to 60 minutes, or until toothpick inserted in center comes
out clean. Turn out on wire rack to cool. Serve with cheese spread.
Makes 1 loaf.

CHEESE SPREAD:
1 package (8 ounces) cream
  cheese, softened
1/4 cup butter or margarine,
  softened

2 teaspoons powdered sugar
1 tablespoon orange-
  flavored liqueur
1 tablespoon grated lime
  peel

In small mixer bowl, beat cream cheese, butter and powdered
sugar until smooth. Stir in liqueur and grated lime peel. Makes
1¼ cups.

Southwest Dinner Rolls

David Wayne

This is another Zest of the Southwest favorite, invented by David Wayne, who moved to Scottsdale from Canada about a year before the 1987 contest took place. A psychologist who bakes for a hobby, Wayne brought his wife Judy with him to the contest. Judy Wayne, a free-lance food writer, wound up contributing some feature stories to the *Republic* Food section.

▼▼▼▼▼▼▼▼▼▼▼▼▼▼▼▼▼▼▼▼▼

1 teaspoon sugar
1 1/2 cups lukewarm water
1 rounded teaspoon dry yeast
4 cups all-purpose or bread
  flour
1/4 cup vegetable oil

1 tablespoon salt
1 cup sharp Cheddar cheese,
  shredded
2 fresh jalapeño peppers,
  seeded and finely diced

Mix well 1 teaspoon of sugar into half-cup of warm water. Activate yeast by sprinkling on top. Let stand for 8 to 10 minutes.

Place flour in bowl of a food processor. Pour in vegetable oil, salt and yeast-water mixture. Process until mixed. With machine running, pour in remaining cup of water, or enough so that mixture forms a ball. Add Cheddar cheese and jalapeños and turn processor on and off several times, quickly, to lightly mix. Place dough in a large greased bowl. Cover and allow to rise for 1½ hours or until doubled in bulk.

Punch down dough and divide into 12 equal pieces. Roll each between hands until 10″ long. Tie ends together (as in first part of tying shoes), turn over and place on cookie sheet, which should be either lightly greased or lined with baking parchment. Repeat for remaining dough. Cover with a cloth and let rise for 1 hour in a warm place.

Twenty minutes before baking, preheat oven to 400°. Sprinkle shaped rolls lightly with white flour and bake at 400° for 15 minutes or until brown. Cool on a wire rack and serve with butter. Makes 12 rolls.

Sweet Potato Buttermilk Biscuits

Judy Keller

Judy Keller of Phoenix wrote in her 1986 Festive Favorites submission that her grandmother from Virginia did a lot of traditional Southern baking with foods she had grown. Judy remembered Sweet Potato Biscuits from her grandmother's table at Thanksgiving and Christmas, and she herself serves them during the holidays.

▼▼▼▼▼▼▼▼▼▼▼▼▼▼▼▼▼▼▼▼

2 cups flour
2 tablespoons baking powder
1/2 teaspoon baking soda
1 teaspoon salt
1 tablespoon sugar
1 tablespoon packed brown
** sugar**

1/3 cup vegetable
** shortening**
3/4 cup buttermilk
3/4 cup mashed cooked
** sweet potatoes**

Preheat oven to 450°. Sift together flour, baking powder, baking soda, salt and sugars. Cut in shortening with pastry blender or two knives until mixture resembles coarse corn meal. Combine buttermilk and potatoes and add to mixture, stirring until all ingredients are moistened.

Turn onto floured surface and knead 8 to 10 times. Roll dough to ½" thickness and cut with a 2" biscuit cutter. Bake on lightly greased baking sheet at 450° for 12 minutes. Makes 1½ dozen biscuits.

Sunshine Breakfast Corn Bread

Mary Geisel

Mary Geisel tested Sunshine Breakfast Corn Bread on her family. On the day of the Zest of the Southwest contest in 1987, she said, "We've eaten so much cornbread lately, I'm ready to douse it with rum and give away the leftovers as Christmas fruitcakes!" The Phoenix resident bakes this breakfast bread the old-fashioned way, in a heavy black cast-iron skillet. If you can't find the assorted dried fruit bits, use whatever dried fruit your family likes, such as raisins or chopped apricots.

▼▼▼▼▼▼▼▼▼▼▼▼▼▼▼▼▼▼▼▼▼

2 tablespoons margarine, melted
3/4 cup flour
1/2 cup yellow cornmeal
1 1/2 teaspoons baking powder
1/2 teaspoon salt
1/4 teaspoon nutmeg
1/2 cup assorted dried fruit bits

1 tablespoon sugar
2 eggs, separated
1/2 cup milk
1/2 cup whole kernel corn
1/2 cup Cheddar or Monterey Jack cheese, grated
4 pieces bacon, cooked and crumbled

Generously oil 8" or 9" black cast-iron skillet with melted margarine and heat in oven at 425° while combining the ingredients.

Combine flour, cornmeal, baking powder, salt, nutmeg, fruit and sugar. Set aside. In a separate, smaller bowl, beat egg whites until peaks form. Set aside.

In medium bowl, blend milk, egg yolks, corn and cheese. Combine milk mixture with dry ingredients, then fold in egg whites.

Remove hot pan from oven, handling carefully. Sprinkle bacon over bottom of pan before adding dough mixture. Spread dough evenly to edges. Bake at 425° for 20 minutes. Carefully turn out on rack. Serve warm with butter. Makes 4 servings.

Chorizo Quick Bread

Mary E. Field

A nurse who lives in Strawberry, Mary E. Field, won in the Breads category of the 1987 Zest of the Southwest contest with this Chorizo Quick Bread. She said then that a friend in California gave her a recipe which called for pepperoni. She substituted chorizo, the spicy Mexican sausage, and added cumin, brown sugar and Parmesan cheese to come up with a winner.

▼▼▼▼▼▼▼▼▼▼▼▼▼▼▼▼▼▼▼▼▼

8 ounces chorizo
3 cups flour
4 tablespoons grated
  Parmesan cheese
3 tablespoons brown sugar
1 1/2 tablespoons baking
  powder
1/4 teaspoon ground cumin

1/2 teaspoon salt
1/4 teaspoon baking soda
1 package (8 ounces) cream
  cheese, room temperature
1 cup milk
2 eggs
1/3 cup melted margarine

Preheat oven to 375°. Crumble chorizo into a skillet and cook, stirring over medium heat until brown and crisp. Lift with slotted spoon to paper towels. Drain thoroughly.

In a large bowl, combine flour, Parmesan cheese, sugar, baking powder, cumin, salt and baking soda. In another large bowl, beat cream cheese until smooth. Stir in milk. Add eggs, one at a time, beating well. Stir in margarine and chorizo. Add to flour mixture and stir until moistened.

Spoon batter into a greased 9″ by 5″ loaf pan. Bake in 375° oven until bread browns, about 55 minutes. Cool in pan on rack for 10 to 15 minutes, then turn out onto rack.

After bread is cool, wrap in foil. Store at room temperature for one day. May be frozen. To serve, thaw wrapped. Uncover and heat at 350° for 15 minutes. Makes 12 servings.

Bolillos (Mexican Hard Rolls)

Eleanor Haire

Bolillos, the Mexican hard rolls shaped like fat little footballs, freeze wonderfully. Use this beautifully written recipe from Eleanor Haire of Phoenix when you have a little time to spend in the kitchen. This was from the 1982 A Taste of Arizona contest. Eleanor points out that the temperature of the water to be combined with the yeast at the beginning of the recipe is vital to predictable bread baking. She used a microwave and microwave thermometer for good results. She also used French bread pans for round, plump shapes.

▼▼▼▼▼▼▼▼▼▼▼▼▼▼▼▼▼▼▼▼

4 to 5 cups sifted unbleached flour, divided	**1/2 tablespoon salt**
1 package active dry yeast	**1 tablespoon shortening**
1 1/4 cups water	**Yellow cornmeal**
1/2 tablespoon sugar	**1 egg white**
	1 tablespoon water

In a large mixer bowl, combine 2 cups of flour and the yeast. In a separate bowl, combine water, sugar, salt and shortening; heat to 115°.

Add the heated mixture to the dry ingredients and beat at high speed for 3 minutes, scraping the bowl at 1-minute intervals. Add enough of the remaining flour to form a soft dough. Knead by hand, or in an electric mixer with a dough hook, for 10 to 12 minutes, until smooth.

Place the kneaded dough in a greased bowl, turning once to grease the surface of the dough. Cover with plastic wrap and let rise for about 1 hour, until doubled. Set covered dough in a warm, draft-free place. If the dough rises before you are ready to shape it, just punch it down, cover it up and let it rise again.

When dough has doubled, punch it down, divide it into 3 equal portions and let it rest 10 minutes, covered.

Roll each portion of dough into a 12" by 5" rectangle. Beginning at the long side, roll tightly, sealing well with the finger tips as you roll. Cut each roll into ¾" pieces. Pull the ends of each piece of dough into points to form an oval-shaped roll. Place each roll on a greased baking sheet that has been sprinkled with yellow cornmeal.

Make a ¼" deep slit lengthwise in the top of each roll. Beat the egg white with water and use half the mixture to brush tops and sides of the rolls. Cover with a damp cloth, being careful not to let the cloth touch the rolls. Let rise about 1 hour, until doubled.

Preheat oven to 375°. Place a pan of boiling water on the floor of the oven. Bake the rolls for 15 minutes. Brush again with egg-white mixture and bake an additional 10 minutes, or until golden. Cool completely on wire racks. Package in heavy-duty freezer bags and freeze.

When ready to serve, place thawed rolls on the oven rack and heat at 350° for 5 to 10 minutes, until crust is nicely crisp. Makes 9 rolls.

Peanut Butter Bread

Candace Unglesby

Even if you never bake, you can successfully whip out this nutritious, good-tasting bread, flavored with a favorite — peanut butter. The oats and cornmeal give it a wonderful texture. This appeared in our 1984 Healthy Appetites supplement, courtesy of Candace Unglesby. This one has all my favorite recipe attributes: it goes together in a wink, requires ingredients you probably have around the house already and earns raves from tasters.

▼▼▼▼▼▼▼▼▼▼▼▼▼▼▼▼▼▼▼

1 cup whole wheat flour
1/2 cup quick-cooking
   rolled oats
1/2 cup yellow cornmeal
1/2 cup dry milk powder
1/2 cup sugar

3 teaspoons baking powder
2/3 cup peanut butter
1 egg
1 1/2 cups 2 percent-fat
   milk

Preheat oven to 350°. Combine flour, oats, cornmeal, milk powder, sugar and baking powder. Mix well. Using a pastry blender, cut in peanut butter.

Mix together egg and milk. Add to flour mixture. Blend well. Pour into greased and floured 9" by 5" by 3" loaf pan. Bake at 350° for 70 minutes. Cool and remove from pan. Makes 1 loaf.

Mexican Bread Puffs

Deniece May

Of all the Southwestern ingredients people used in the 1987 Zest of the Southwest contest recipes, Deniece May was the only person to get to the finals using taco seasoning mix! Deniece, from Phoenix, told the judges, "This recipe came to mind when I was preparing dinner and didn't have time to make sopapillas." Like sopapillas, they are crusty on the outside and soft in the middle.

▼▼▼▼▼▼▼▼▼▼▼▼▼▼▼▼▼▼▼▼

2 cups flour
1/2 teaspoon salt
3 tablespoons baking powder
1 teaspoon sugar

1 teaspoon taco seasoning
    mix
1 cup cold water
Oil for frying

Mix dry ingredients. Add water and stir dough until all of the flour is incorporated. Dough should be sticky.

Heat 1″ of oil in a skillet. Drop dough by heaping tablespoons two at a time into hot oil. Fry until golden brown. Drain on paper towels and serve right away. Bread puffs will be crusty on the outside but soft in the middle. Makes 12 puffs.

Tomato-Cilantro Bread

Janet Gould

I'll never forget the first time I tasted fresh cilantro, at my friend Wendy Govier's house. I was hooked. Soon I learned that people either love or loathe this pungent herb, which goes by many names in different ethnic cuisines. American cookbooks from the East always call it "fresh coriander." I prefer the Spanish designation, and I never tire of it chopped into fresh salsa.

This moist, colorful bread was submitted by Janet Gould of Scottsdale for the Zest of the Southwest cookoff. It is further enlivened by a zingy spread of cream cheese laced with jalapeños. If you want less zing in the spread, be sure to eliminate the chilie pepper seeds. This recipe uses a food processor but can be made without one. Use a blender to puree the cilantro, green onion, tomatoes and tomato paste.

▼▼▼▼▼▼▼▼▼▼▼▼▼▼▼▼▼▼▼▼

2 cups flour
1 teaspoon baking soda
1 tablespoon baking powder
1 teaspoon salt
1 teaspoon ground cumin
1/2 cup fresh cilantro leaves,
  closely packed

1 whole green onion, cut into
  1" pieces
3 tomatoes, seeded and
  quartered
1 tablespoon tomato paste
3/4 cup sugar
3 large eggs

Preheat oven to 350°. Place flour, baking soda, baking powder, salt and cumin in work bowl with metal blade and process for 2 seconds. Move dry ingredients to another bowl.

Process cilantro and green onion for 5 seconds. Add tomatoes and tomato paste and process until tomatoes are pureed, about 10 seconds. Add sugar and process for 30 seconds, stopping to scrape down sides of bowl. Add eggs and process for 1 minute, or until mixture becomes fluffy. Return dry ingredients to processor and combine by turning machine on and off 4 to 5 times until mixture is just incorporated.

Pour mixture into greased and floured 9" by 5" loaf pan. Spread the mixture evenly and bake at 350° for 45 minutes or until browned. Let the bread cool in pan for 10 minutes and turn onto wire rack to cool completely.

This bread is great alone or with butter. For a sensational treat, spread the bread with Jalapeño Cream Cheese.

Jalapeño Cream Cheese:
  4 ounces cream cheese
  1 jalapeño, finely chopped
    (vary to taste)

Whip cream cheese until soft and mix in chopped jalapeño.

Secret Center Nut Bread

Gloria Gorce

"I always enjoy people's surprise when they find the cream cheese already there!" wrote Gloria Gorce of Phoenix about her entry in the 1986 Festive Favorites contest, where she was a finalist with this intriguing bread.

▼▼▼▼▼▼▼▼▼▼▼▼▼▼▼▼▼▼▼▼

FILLING:
2 packages (3 ounces each)
    cream cheese, softened
1 egg
2 tablespoons flour
1 tablespoon grated orange
    peel
3/4 cup sugar

BREAD:
2/3 cup honey
2/3 cup milk
2 1/2 cups flour
1/3 cup sugar
1 teaspoon soda
1 teaspoon salt
1/2 cup shortening
1 egg
1 cup chopped nuts

Preheat oven to 325°. Combine cream cheese, egg, 2 tablespoons flour, grated orange peel and sugar in a small mixing bowl. Blend at low speed until well mixed. Set aside.

To make the bread, combine honey and milk in large mixer bowl. Add flour, sugar, soda, salt, shortening and egg. Blend at low speed just until smooth, about 1 minute.
Scrape sides of bowl frequently.

Stir in nuts. Spread half of batter in greased and floured 9" by 5" by 3" loaf pan. Pour filling over batter. Carefully spoon remaining batter over filling and gently spread. Bake for 1 hour and 15 minutes to 1 hour and 25 minutes. Cool 15 minutes. Remove from pan. Cool on wire rack. Wrap tightly in aluminum foil and store in refrigerator. Makes one loaf.

Fiesta Bread

Sylvia Schmitt

This was Sylvia Schmitt's first entry in a cooking contest, but was by no means her last. The Glendale resident won $150 in the 1982 Taste of Arizona cookoff, and has since made a hobby of entering cooking contests, winning on the national level several times.

Although she's Italian, Sylvia placed first in the Mexican category with this bread, her adaptation of an Italian favorite. The spiciness of the bread depends on the chorizo, which can be mild or hot, beef or pork, depending on your taste. (*Note:* To quick-thaw frozen bread dough, microwave the loaf for 10 minutes on medium-low/defrost, turning several times.)

▼▼▼▼▼▼▼▼▼▼▼▼▼▼▼▼▼▼▼▼▼

1 loaf frozen bread dough
1 cup Longhorn Cheddar cheese, shredded
1/2 cup chorizo (Mexican sausage), cooked and drained

1 can (3 1/2 or 4 ounces) chopped green chilies, drained
1 egg, beaten
Melted butter

Allow frozen dough to thaw. Using greased fingers, stretch dough on a greased cookie sheet into a 6" by 12" rectangle. Set aside.

Prepare filling by combining cheese, chorizo, chilies and egg. Spread filling on top of dough and then roll, jellyroll-fashion. Place rolled dough on a greased cookie sheet, seam side down, and let rise at room temperature until double in size.

Preheat oven to 375°. Brush top of loaf with melted butter. Bake at 375° for 20 minutes. Makes 1 loaf, about 8 servings.

Fig Date Bread

Ida "Mickey" Plumb

Everybody who has a fig tree in the desert is always looking for another recipe using this ancient fruit. Not only is this bread quick and simple to make, it yields three or four small loaves that make terrific gifts. Ida "Mickey" Plumb of Phoenix sent this in for our 1987 Zest of the Southwest contest. (*Hint:* If you have a problem chopping sticky dates or figs, dip your knife blade in flour every now and then. Or use a pair of kitchen shears to snip them into bits.)

▼▼▼▼▼▼▼▼▼▼▼▼▼▼▼▼▼▼▼

1 1/2 cups chopped fresh figs	2 1/8 cups flour
1 1/4 cups chopped dates	1 teaspoon baking soda
1/2 cup butter or margarine	1/2 teaspoon salt
1 cup sugar minus 2 tablespoons	1/4 teaspoon nutmeg
2 eggs, beaten	1/2 teaspoon cinnamon
	1 cup chopped nuts

Preheat oven to 350°. Put figs and dates in pan and heat until hot. Set aside. In a large mixing bowl, using an electric mixer, beat butter and sugar together until fluffy. Add beaten eggs. Beat in 1 cup flour, baking soda, salt, nutmeg and cinnamon. Add figs and dates and blend well by hand. Add second cup flour and mix until well-blended. Add nuts.

Grease and flour 4 loaf pans (3¼" by 6") or 3 loaf pans (3½" by 7½"). Pour equal amounts of batter into pans. Bake at 350° for about 55 minutes. Test by inserting toothpick near center. Pick should come out clean. Let cool briefly in pans, then turn out onto racks to cool. Makes 3 or 4 loaves.

Pumpkin Corn Bread

Rebecca Keck

The wonderful combination of flavors in this unusual cornbread persuaded our 1986 panel of judges to award the Bread category prize to Rebecca Keck. She lived in Clarkdale when she entered that year, but was a Phoenix resident when she made it to the finals of the 1988 contest.

In 1986 we printed contestants' comments with their recipes, to let readers know how these dishes came to be Festive Favorites, our contest theme. Rebecca wrote, "I found this recipe while working at the South Rim of the Grand Canyon. I knew it would make a wonderful treat for my boss. His name was Buck Valentine, and he had mentioned he liked corn bread. This is the only reason I would have ever noticed this combination. Since I have been married it has been a family favorite any time I fix it, particularly during the holidays. This can be made ahead and frozen, then reheated just before serving."

▼▼▼▼▼▼▼▼▼▼▼▼▼▼▼▼▼▼▼▼▼

1 1/4 cups flour (whole-wheat blend)
1 tablespoon baking powder
1/2 teaspoon salt
1/2 teaspoon grated nutmeg
1/4 teaspoon ground mace
3/4 cup yellow cornmeal

2/3 cup light brown sugar
2 tablespoons honey
1/4 cup melted butter
2 eggs, lightly beaten
3/4 cup pumpkin puree
2/3 cup buttermilk

Preheat oven to 350°. Mix flour, baking powder, salt, nutmeg and mace. Stir in cornmeal. Combine brown sugar, honey and butter in a bowl and mix well. Add eggs, pumpkin and buttermilk. Stir the liquid ingredients into the dry ones, stirring only long enough to mix well. Place the mixture in a greased 8″ square baking pan and bake for 40 to 45 minutes or until firm.
Serve warm. Makes 6 to 10 servings.

Mango Bread

Denelle Cornett

This bread, from Denelle Cornett, combines the tropical favor of mangoes with the homey texture of a quick sweet bread, similar to banana bread. The Phoenix resident submitted this to the 1987 Zest of the Southwest contest. Mangos are becoming more and more common in supermarkets, especially since exotic produce began to proliferate five years ago. Recently, I've found them displayed in a way that helps solve the oldest problem about mangos: How to eat one without wearing it.

Smart produce managers slit them in half, remove the seed, and cut the pulp still on the peel into neat hatchmarks. Then they pop the peel inside out, so the pulp stands out, ready to be eaten or used in a recipe. (The best place to eat a mango? In the bathtub.)

▼▼▼▼▼▼▼▼▼▼▼▼▼▼▼▼▼▼▼

2 1/2 cups finely diced mango (about 2 large)	1/2 teaspoon salt
	1 1/4 cups sugar
1 tablespoon lemon juice	3 eggs
2 cups flour	3/4 cup vegetable oil
1 1/2 teaspoons cinnamon	1 cup chopped walnuts
1 1/2 teaspoons baking soda	

Grease and flour two 9" by 5" loaf pans. Preheat oven to 325°. Sprinkle diced mangoes with lemon juice, and set aside to marinate. In a large bowl, mix the flour, cinnamon, baking soda, salt and sugar. In another bowl, beat the eggs and oil together. Blend the mangoes into the egg and oil mixture.

To complete the batter, mix the mango-egg mixture with the flour mixture. Add the walnuts. Blend well.

Pour the batter into the two pans, dividing equally. Bake at 325° for 50 to 60 minutes. Makes two loaves.

VEGETABLES AND SIDE DISHES

This is the chapter where vegetables are found, but it's also home for those wonderful complex carbohydrates we should eat more often. Rice and beans, mainstay of global cuisines, appear here in assorted creative guises.

Eric's Lucky Black-Eyed Peas is one example. It won the 1986 Festive Favorites contest hands down. Young bachelor winner Eric Gironda grew up in New Orleans, and lordy, could he cook! Eric had never even written down a recipe until he entered our contest, but the final result had the judges sneaking second helpings. The spicy dish immediately became a favorite.

Eric will introduce you to black-eyed peas if you have never had them. Mary Sue Tuzzio, another grand-prize winner, will help you make the acquaintance of tomatillos, a special Southwestern ingredient. Never had hominy, or *no-palltos*? There are recipes for those, too.

Of course you'll find old favorites in new get-ups: potatoes, onions, corn, sweet potatoes, brussels sprouts, lots of green chilies. And for special occasions, try the Holiday Vegetable Platter: an elegant carrot ring filled with French peas and surrounded with steamed cauliflower.

Brussels Sprouts, California-Style

Joan Bulkley

Brussels sprouts with grapes and wine? Try it. It's the favorite holiday vegetable of the family of Joan Bulkley of Humbolt, who learned to cook with wine when she lived in California. In the 1986 Festive Favorites contest, Joan noted that this is good with wild duck, turkey or venison.

▼▼▼▼▼▼▼▼▼▼▼▼▼▼▼▼▼▼▼▼▼▼

**1 pound fresh brussels
  sprouts
1 cup chablis wine**

**3/4 cup small white seedless
  grapes
Butter
Salt and pepper to taste**

Cut stems from the sprouts and remove wilted outer leaves. Heat chablis in a 1½-quart saucepan. When wine reaches boiling point, add sprouts. Reduce heat and simmer, uncovered, until barely tender, about 10 minutes. Remove from heat.

Season with butter, salt and pepper. Add grapes. Toss gently. Reheat before serving. Makes 4 to 6 servings.

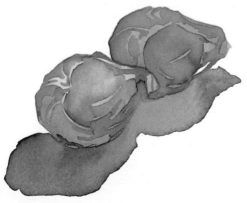

Sweet Potato "Empanaditas" (Little Turnovers)

Marlys Walrath

Marlys Walrath of Phoenix enters cooking contests as a hobby, and this creation took her to The Ranch for the 1987 Zest of the Southwest contest as a finalist. She said she creates recipes by using whatever ingredients she has on hand — luckily, she has an adventurous husband.

Again, those wonderful flour tortillas show up, this time slathered with a spiced sweet-potato filling. They are baked and brushed with melted butter, Parmesan cheese and chili powder. (Those last three ingredients are often seen in the summer in combination, when they are offered at border fairs with a popular treat, corn on the cob. Ears of sweet corn are grilled in the husks, which are then pulled down and wrapped in paper to form a handle. Dunked in butter, the corn is handed over to the hungry eater, who adds cheese and chili powder to taste.)

▼▼▼▼▼▼▼▼▼▼▼▼▼▼▼▼▼▼▼▼▼

3 cups sweet potatoes, cooked and mashed
8 tablespoons butter or margarine, melted, divided
1/4 cup orange juice
1/4 teaspoon cinnamon
1 tablespoon sugar

2 eggs, each beaten separately
1 tablespoon oil
12 flour tortillas (6" to 7" diameter)
3 tablespoons Parmesan cheese
1/2 tablespoon chili powder

Preheat oven to 425°. In a large mixing bowl, place sweet potatoes, 6 tablespoons butter, orange juice, cinnamon, sugar and 1 beaten egg. Blend well.

Combine oil with other beaten egg in a small bowl. Brush each tortilla with oil-egg mixture on both sides. Let soften.

Spread ¼ cup of sweet-potato filling over one side of each tortilla, leaving a ¼" border. Fold in half, then in half again, to form a wedge.

Use all the tortillas. Arrange "turnovers," overlapping slightly, on a buttered ovenproof platter or baking dish (about 10" by 6" by 1½"). Brush with remaining 2 tablespoons melted butter and sprinkle with Parmesan cheese and chili powder.

Bake until cheese is melted, 8 to 10 minutes. Makes 12 servings.

Green Chili Corn Fritters

Lary Groen

Lary Groen of Sedona updated an old favorite, corn fritters, for the 1987 Zest of the Southest contest. If you don't have onion powder, substitute a tablespoon of the real thing, very finely chopped.

▼▼▼▼▼▼▼▼▼▼▼▼▼▼▼▼▼▼

3 cups fresh corn cut from the cob (about 3 ears)
1 can (4 ounces) chopped green chilies, drained
4 eggs
1/2 teaspoon salt

1/8 teaspoon onion powder
1/2 cup plus 2 tablespoons flour
1 teaspoon corn oil
1 teaspoon sugar
Corn oil for cooking

Put corn in a 2-quart bowl (you should have about 3 cups). Add chilies, eggs, salt, onion powder, flour, 1 teaspoon corn oil and sugar; mix thoroughly until well-blended.

In a heavy 10″ skillet, heat ⅛″ of corn oil until it ripples slightly. Spoon half the batter into skillet to form 4 fritters. These should be about ⅝″ thick. Cook over medium heat until tops are somewhat dry and edges are golden brown, about 4 minutes. With a spatula, turn fritters and cook until sides are brown and crisp. Repeat with rest of batter. Makes 8 to 10 fritters.

Tomatilla and Four-Pepper Compote

Mary Sue Tuzzio

This zesty dish can be served on the side, or it can be used as a topping on sautéed fish, pork tenderloin, or chicken. Its versatility and flavor won more money for Mary Sue Tuzzio than for any other contestant in the history of our contests. In the Zest of the Southwest cookoff in 1987, she won $250 as the Side Dishes winner, and $1,000 for best-of-contest grand prize.

The Chandler resident said she had just worked out the recipe to her satisfaction when she noticed the *Republic* was sponsoring the contest. She typed and mailed the recipe and totally forgot about it, until she got a phone call asking her to be a finalist. Tomatillos are covered in a papery husk, which is removed before cooking and must be well-washed, since they grow close to the ground.

▼▼▼▼▼▼▼▼▼▼▼▼▼▼▼▼▼▼▼▼

4 tablespoons butter
1 medium red or yellow
onion, chopped
1 large red bell pepper,
seeded and thinly sliced
in strips
1 large green bell pepper,
seeded and thinly sliced
in strips
1 large fresh Anaheim chilie
pepper, seeded and
chopped

2 fresh jalapeño peppers,
seeded and chopped
4 cloves garlic, finely
chopped
Salt to taste
1/4 teaspoon cayenne pepper
(optional)
1/2 teaspoon ground cumin
1/3 cup chicken broth
6 fresh tomatillos, husked,
washed and quartered
1/3 cup fresh cilantro,
coarsely chopped

In a 12″ or 14″ skillet, melt butter over medium heat. Add onion and sauté briefly until limp, about 2 minutes. Add sliced and chopped peppers and garlic; sauté, stirring occasionally, until peppers just begin to soften, about 5 minutes.

Add salt, cayenne and cumin. Stir well. Raise heat to medium-high and add chicken broth and tomatillos. Heat until broth comes to a boil and tomatillos are heated through, 3 to 4 minutes. Remove from heat and stir in fresh cilantro.

Serve immediately as a side dish, or over sautéed orange roughy, halibut, swordfish or boneless breast of chicken. Makes 4 servings.

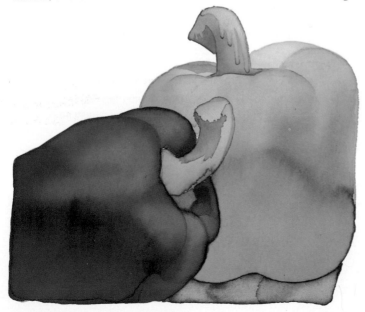

Holiday Vegetable Platter

Marilyn T. Anderson

The competition in the 1986 Festive Favorites contest was especially tight in the Special Vegetables category. This was one of the reasons. Phoenix resident Marilyn T. Anderson said this dish has been a subject of much glowing discussion through the years, because it's a classic method of serving favorite vegetables in a unique fashion, pleasing everyone.

▼▼▼▼▼▼▼▼▼▼▼▼▼▼▼▼▼▼▼▼

CARROT RING:
1 1/2 cups (3 sticks) butter, room temperature
1 cup firmly packed brown sugar
4 eggs, separated
3 cups finely grated raw carrots (about 1 pound)
2 tablespoons cold water
2 tablespoons lemon juice
2 cups flour
1 teaspoon baking soda
2 teaspoons baking powder
1 teaspoon salt
1/4 cup bread crumbs
FRENCH PEAS:
6 tablespoons butter

1/4 cup finely chopped lettuce
1 1/2 pounds frozen tiny peas, unthawed, or shelled fresh peas
1/4 cup minced shallots or white part of green onion
1 large sprig parsley
2 to 4 teaspoons sugar
1 teaspoon salt
1/8 teaspoon white pepper
STEAMED CAULIFLOWER:
1 large cauliflower
1 teaspoon salt
GARNISH:
Paprika
Parsley sprigs

First, make carrot ring:

Preheat oven to 350°. Cream butter and brown sugar. Add yolks and beat until thick. Add carrots, water, lemon juice, flour, baking soda, baking powder and salt. Mix thoroughly. Beat egg whites until stiff peaks form. Fold into carrot mixture.

Generously oil a 3-quart ring mold; dust with bread crumbs. Turn carrot mixture into mold. Bake 1 hour. Remove from oven and allow to cool 3 minutes before loosening edges with dull-edged knife. Turn onto heated round serving platter.

Carrot Ring ingredients may be combined a day in advance. Bake just before serving.

To make French peas:

Melt butter in 3-quart saucepan. Place lettuce on top of butter. Add peas, shallots, parsley, sugar, salt and pepper. Simmer covered, stirring occasionally, until peas are tender, 10 to 15 minutes. Remove parsley.

To make steamed cauliflower:

Trim heavy outside leaves from cauliflower. Cut cauliflower into florets. Place in steamer or colander over boiling water. Steam covered until crisp-tender, about 15 minutes. Sprinkle with salt. Just before serving, dust with paprika.

To serve:

Place baked carrot ring on a heated round serving platter. Fill center of ring with carefully drained French peas. Surround outer edge with steamed cauliflower lightly sprinkled with paprika. Garnish with parsley sprigs. Makes 12 servings.

Hopi Corn Stew

Ginny Seaton

Ginny Seaton of Phoenix won the Indian category of the 1982 Taste of Arizona contest with this recipe that she got from a friend on the Gila River Indian Reservation. It's a good way to use a bit of extra roast beef or ground beef. Ginny noted that this is excellent served with hard Indian (sometimes called Squaw) bread.

▼▼▼▼▼▼▼▼▼▼▼▼▼▼▼▼▼▼

**1 cup roast beef or ground
  beef, chopped
1 tablespoon shortening
Salt and pepper to taste
2 cups fresh corn, cut from
  cobs**

**1 cup zucchini squash, cubed
2 cups plus 2 tablespoons
  water
2 tablespoons cornmeal**

Heat shortening in a large heavy skillet. Brown meat and add salt and pepper to taste.

Add squash, corn and 2 cups water; simmer about 30 minutes, or until vegetables are almost tender.

In a cup, stir together cornmeal and 2 tablespoons water to make a paste. Stir thickener into stew; stir about 5 minutes to prevent sticking. Makes 4 servings.

Verdolagas

Alicia Jacobs

Phoenix resident Alicia Jacobs entered this recipe in the 1982 Taste of Arizona contest, and the judges—all chefs—were mightily intrigued. They handed her the grand prize money and suddenly everybody wanted to know where Alicia got this unusual verdolagas. Answer: Her own backyard.

Commonly known as purslane, the wild green grows as a weed but is also cultivated in some places. It can be used in soups, salads or as any other green is used. The leaves are round and thickish. Jacobs said to use only the tips of the stems and the larger leaves, and to wash it all very well. Although the taste would be different, fresh spinach or greens such as collards could be substituted for the purslane.

**1/2 pound verdolagas
(purslane), leaves and
tender tips only
2 tablespoons oil
1/2 pound pork chops or
ribs, boned and cubed**

**1/4 medium onion, chopped
1 garlic clove, chopped
1 tomato, chopped
1/2 teaspoon chicken
bouillon granules**

Steam verdolgas as you would spinach. Set aside.

Heat 1 tablespoon oil in a large skillet. Brown pork cubes and
set aside.

Heat remaining 1 tablespoon oil in large skillet. Sauté onion,
garlic and tomato. Stir in bouillon granules. Add browned meat and
steamed verdologas. Simmer for 15 to 20 minutes. Makes 5
servings.

Sa'auba (Tortillas and Onions)

Margo J. Menson

Margo J. Menson of Sacaton, on the Gila River Indian Reservation,
said this is an old, basically Pima dish that has retained its popularity because it is quick, easy to prepare and tasty. Menson learned
to cook from her mother and grandmother. Her efforts kept our
1982 judges in a long debate—this nearly won in the Taste of Arizona contest. It's a filling breakfast dish.

▼▼▼▼▼▼▼▼▼▼▼▼▼▼▼▼▼▼▼▼

**2 to 3 large flour tortillas
1 medium-sized onion
2 to 3 tablespoons lard**

**Shredded longhorn cheese
(about 1/2 cup, or to
taste)
Chopped green chilies (about
1/2 cup, or to taste)**

In a heavy 10″ skillet, melt lard; let it get very hot. Peel and halve
onion lengthwise and slice moderately thin, about ⅛″

Add to hot fat and fry until onion separates and is translucent.
Tear tortillas into pieces about 2″ to 3″ across. Add to onion and fry
until soft, evenly mixing them with onion.

Serve for breakfast from skillet or covered dish, sprinkled with
grated longhorn cheese and/or diced green chilies. Makes 6
servings.

Savory Nopalitos

Virginia Yates

Nopalitos are the tender pads of prickly pear cactus, a desert specialty that has become more popular through the years of the Southwestern food focus. It is now relatively easy to find fresh nopalitos, although they have long been available, canned, in Mexican markets. Virginia Yates of Paradise Valley used canned nopalitos to create this dish for the 1987 Zest of the Southwest contest.

▼▼▼▼▼▼▼▼▼▼▼▼▼▼▼▼▼▼▼▼

6 strips bacon, sliced
1/2 medium onion, minced
3 cloves garlic, pressed
1/4 teaspoon salt
2 cups canned nopalitos
(cactus pads, such as
Embasa brand) rinsed and
throughly drained

1/4 teaspoon freshly ground
black pepper
1 teaspoon lemon juice
1/4 teaspoon lemon zest

Brown bacon in heavy saucepan until crisp. Drain all fat except 2 tablespoons. Add onion and garlic; sauté until onions are translucent. Add salt, nopalitos, pepper, lemon juice and lemon zest. Heat thoroughly and serve. Makes 4 servings.

Easy Mexican Hominy

Sammie Caywood

Sammie Caywood of Casa Grande submitted this for the 1987 Zest of the Southwest cookoff, and it lives up to its name—easy, simple and delicious. It's also a good substitute for Spanish rice on your Mexican menu.

I once wrote a food story in answer to the question: Just what IS hominy, anyway? I knew hominy had some history, because my mother remembers her grandmother cooking it in a big black iron pot and canning the result. Come to find out, hominy goes back to the Indians, who processed corn this way and dried it. Some parts of the country call hominy "samp." Southerners, of course, love their hominy grits. Just what hominy grits ARE is another story....

▼▼▼▼▼▼▼▼▼▼▼▼▼▼▼▼▼▼▼▼

4 slices bacon, chopped
1 small onion, chopped
1 can (29 ounces) yellow or
   white hominy, drained
1 teaspoon red chili powder

Salt to taste (optional)
2 cans (8 ounces each)
   tomato sauce
1 can (4 ounces) chopped
   green chilies (optional)

In a skillet over medium heat, cook chopped bacon until done but not crisp. Add chopped onion and chopped green chilies if using. Cook 5 minutes, or until slightly done. Add drained hominy, chili powder and salt; stir, add tomato sauce. Cover pan and simmer over low heat about 20 minutes, stirring occasionally. Serve hot. Makes 6 servings.

Eric's Lucky Black-Eyed Peas

Eric Gironda

In the 1986 Festive Favorites contest, entrants had to explain what made this dish qualify as a holiday dish. Eric Gironda of Phoenix wrote, "At New Year's, it is considered good luck to eat black-eyed peas in Louisiana, and most families serve them as an appetizer on this holiday. It is also considered very good luck to get a piece of bay leaf in your peas, which is why you don't remove them, but please don't eat them. Black-eyed peas are also eaten as a main course, but they are lucky only on New Year's Eve. They freeze very well, also. You may cut the recipe in half, but I gar-on-tee you'll be sorry."

Throughout the South, the venerated black-eye is consumed on New Year's Day, often flavored with pork. The smoked ham hocks and sausages in this dish give it a superb flavor. *Warning:* these babies are SPICY. If you and your family or friends don't have asbestos palates, reduce the cayenne, Tabasco and black pepper by at least half the first time you make this dish.

▼▼▼▼▼▼▼▼▼▼▼▼▼▼▼▼▼▼▼▼

1 medium onion, chopped
1 teaspoon oil
2 pounds dry black-eyed peas
2 pounds smoked ham hocks (or 3 large)
1 1/2 pounds good-quality smoked sausage
10 large cloves garlic (or 20 small)
2 large bay leaves

1/4 cup chopped fresh parsley
1 tablespoon cayenne pepper (or less, to taste)
1 tablespoon Tabasco pepper sauce (or less, to taste)
2 tablespoons freshly ground black pepper (or less, to taste)
Salt to taste

Heat oil in a large soup pot and brown chopped onion. Set aside. Sort peas carefully to remove stones and dirt, rinse well. Dump peas in pot with onion; add ham hocks, bay leaves, parsley, cayenne, black pepper (don't use pre-ground pepper), Tabasco sauce and half of the garlic. Cover with water; cook on high until just boiling, and turn down heat to low, to simmer. Add water as necessary to keep covered. Stir occasionally.

Cut smoked sausage into ¾" slices, then cut slices in quarters. After peas have simmered for about 1½ hours, remove ham hocks and set aside to cool. Add sausage and remaining garlic. (It is not necessary to cut up garlic. It'll fall apart—and your hands won't smell.) When ham hocks have cooled, remove and discard skin. Remove meat from bones and gristle from meat. Shred meat and return to pot. Return large bones to pot. Cook on low for another hour or until peas melt in your mouth, keeping them covered with water and stirring as needed to prevent sticking. Peas should be like a bean soup with plenty of liquid, or you can smash up a few peas to create a smooth, thick consistency. Add salt if needed. Remove bay leaves, tear in half, and return to peas. Remove bones.

Serve with a dash of vinegar (malt if possible) and steamed white rice, to cool the palate (optional). Makes 30 ½-cup servings.

Calabacitas

Rebecca Bontrager

Calabacitas means "little squash" in Spanish, and this tasty dish has become more well-known since a popular downtown restaurant, Norman's Fina Cocina, includes it on the menu. Rebecca Bontrager of Phoenix brought this when she was named a finalist in the 1982 Taste of Arizona contest. Adding a diced tomato or a tablespoon of pimento gives this dish an extra dab of color and flavor.

▼▼▼▼▼▼▼▼▼▼▼▼▼▼▼▼▼▼▼▼▼

1 tablespoon butter	1/2 clove garlic, chopped
4 medium zucchini squash, cubed (about 4 cups)	1/2 teaspoon salt
	1/8 teaspoon pepper
1 medium onion, chopped	1 can (10 ounces) corn
1 fresh jalapeño pepper, seeded and diced	1/2 cup jack or American cheese, grated

Melt butter in medium saucepan or skillet. Sauté squash with onion, jalapeño pepper and garlic. Add salt, pepper and corn; cook over medium heat 10 minutes. Sprinkle cheese over top; lower heat, and cover 2 to 4 minutes, until cheese melts. Makes 6 to 8 servings.

Potato Balls

Patricia A. Underhill

Patricia Underhill's recipe was another reason for the stiff competition in the 1986 Special Vegetables category. Here is how the Scottsdale resident described this Festive Favorite: "This recipe was one originally prepared by me for a family holiday engagement dinner for my then to-be-husband and myself. My [future] husband was rather unsure of my cooking talents in those days...and was quite surprised by this dish and a few others. It has been a family favorite for our holiday meals for the past 25 years and lends itself very well as an accompaniment to beef and pork roasts or roast goose. A variety of cheeses and herbs may be substituted in this recipe."

▼▼▼▼▼▼▼▼▼▼▼▼▼▼▼▼▼▼▼▼▼

4 medium potatoes
2 teaspoons salt, divided
2 tablespoons butter
1/2 cup milk
1/4 teaspoon white pepper
1 egg yolk
1 tablespoon snipped chives

1/2 pound sharp Cheddar cheese (or cheese of choice)
1/2 cup melted butter
1 cup seasoned bread crumbs (or 1 cup finely crushed corn flakes)
Paprika
Chives

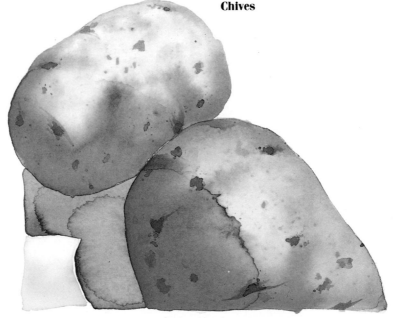

Wash and peel the potatoes. Place in a saucepan with water to cover and 1 teaspoon of salt. Cover and cook until the potatoes are tender but not mushy. Drain potatoes and mash with the butter, milk, remaining salt, pepper, egg yolk and chives. Potatoes should be stiff. Cool thoroughly.

Cut cheese into 1" cubes, shaping cold potatoes around cheese. (Remember, potatoes must be stiff enough to hold their shape around cheese.) Roll balls in melted butter, then in crumbs or corn flakes. Place in shallow muffin pans and bake at 400° until golden brown, about 15 minutes.

When done, dust potato balls lightly with paprika and sprinkle chives over them. Potato balls should be brown and crusty, and the cheese should be soft and melty. Makes 6 to 8 servings.

Nana's Onions in Wine Sauce

Peggy Jordan

Peggy Jordan of Tempe was a contest finalist in 1982 and 1986, both times with recipes that were family favorites. (Her other recipe, Panhellic Western Casserole, is on page 80.) Here is what she wrote about the vegetable category winner in the Festive Favorites cookoff: "Most recipes are changed a bit as they pass from generation to generation. However, Nana's Onions in Wine Sauce is the exact recipe and just as perfect today as it was 50 years ago in Atlanta, Georgia, where it originated in my grandmother's kitchen."

2 pounds tiny boiling onions	1 cup half-and-half
2 cups water	2 tablespoons chopped parsley
1 cup white wine	Dash of white pepper
1/2 teaspoon salt	3 tablespoons grated Parmesan cheese
4 tablespoons butter	
4 tablespoons flour	

Peel away outer skin of onions. In a saucepan, bring to a boil onions, water, wine and salt. Reduce heat; simmer uncovered for 20 minutes. Drain, saving liquid. In a separate saucepan, melt butter. Stir in flour; blend in cream and 1 cup reserved liquid, stirring constantly, until thickened. Add parsley, pepper and onions.

Pour into 1-quart greased casserole dish and sprinkle top with Parmesan cheese. Bake 25 minutes at 375°. Makes 8 servings.

Kentucky Sweet Potatoes

Catherine Calk McCarty

At 102, Catherine Calk McCarty of Phoenix was the oldest finalist we ever had. This was her recipe in the 1986 Festive Favorites contest. She wrote that it always brings back one of her best childhood memories, "a Kentucky holiday with our large family around the dining table, in the late 1800s." Yams may be substituted for sweet potatoes here, she said, but they're not as good.

▼▼▼▼▼▼▼▼▼▼▼▼▼▼▼▼▼▼▼▼

6 medium sweet potatoes
3/4 cup brown sugar
3/4 teaspoon salt, or to taste

1/2 stick butter
1/2 cup Kentucky aged
straight bourbon whiskey
1 teaspoon lemon juice

Choose medium-sized sweet potatoes with smooth skins. Wash well and place in large saucepan. Cover with warm water. Boil, uncovered, until barely done and not mushy. Place in cold water, then quickly remove skins, being careful not to mash them. Cut potatoes lengthwise into ⅜" slices. Place a layer of the sweet potatoes in a shallow 2-quart casserole dish that has been generously buttered. Combine brown sugar and salt. Add dots of butter and some of the brown sugar-salt mixture. Repeat layers until all potatoes are used.

Mix bourbon and lemon juice and pour evenly over the casserole. Bake at 375° until bubbly, about 20 minutes. Makes 8 servings.

Southwestern Rice and Green Chili Pesto

Janet Gould

Creator Janet Gould of Scottsdale uses her green chili pesto in many different dishes, as well as on its own as a dip for tortilla chips. Combined with rice and a few other colorful ingredients, this took her to the finals of the 1987 Zest of the Southwest cookoff at The Ranch.

▼▼▼▼▼▼▼▼▼▼▼▼▼▼▼▼▼▼▼▼

1 tablespoon butter
1 teaspoon salt
3 cups hot, cooked rice
3/4 cup Green Chili Pesto
 (*recipe below*)

1/2 cup corn kernels
2 medium tomatoes, cubed
1/2 cup walnut pieces
1/4 cup cilantro leaves,
 tightly packed

Add butter and salt to cooked rice. Mix in pesto with wooden spoon until well combined. Add corn, tomatoes, walnut pieces and cilantro, reserving a few cilantro leaves for garnish. Makes 6 to 8 servings.

GREEN CHILI PESTO:
1/2 cup grated Parmesan
 cheese
1 1/4 cups chopped fresh
 green chilies, seeded
1/2 cup walnut pieces

2 cloves garlic, chopped
1/2 cup cilantro leaves,
 loosely packed
Juice of 1/2 lime
5 tablespoons olive oil

Place all ingredients except olive oil in food processor. Process 5 seconds. With machine running, add olive oil in a thin stream. Process until finely chopped, about 30 seconds.

MAIN DISHES

The most exciting event in any contest is the dec-
laration of the winner—even though not everyone won, there were seldom any sour grapes
after our recipe contests. All the finalists went
home with aprons and other souvenirs of the
occasion. And although whoever took the grand
prize won the biggest check, category winners
got money, too.

Several recipes in this chapter earned money
for their inventors. In addition to those, I have
tried to select an assortment of entrees suitable
for a variety of situations. No-Title Turkey, for
instance, is perfect for a healthful Sunday-night
supper. Totables for tailgate parties include
French Picnic Pie and Cornish Picnic Pastries.
Want something Southwestern? Look at the recipes for Southwestern Sweet-and-Sour Squealer
or Blue Corn Tamale Pie with Butterfly Guaymas
Shrimp and Goat Cheese. Breast of Chicken with
Zucchini and Mushrooms and Chicken in Parchment both bake in convenient packets and have
negligible amounts of fat. Elegant dinner parties
are sure to be enhanced by Chicken Encanto or
Cheesy Seafood Lasagna Rolls.

Of course, there are recipes for when nothing
else but an Arizona flavor will do. Navajo Tacos
are an all-time favorite; also try Chinle Lamb,
Tortilla Quiche, Green Corn Tamales and Chilaquiles.

You're sure to find your own favorites, just as
I have.

Spiced Cold Corn Beef Brisket

Joedy L. Armstrong

Here is an old-fashioned brisket recipe that may remind some of you of a favorite childhood flavor. Even if the taste is new to you, it's excellent, and the mustard sauce is a treasure itself. Use it with other meats, cheeses or even in salads. The brisket is even better if you make it a day before you plan to serve it. Leftovers are great smothered in barbecue sauce. (This is another recipe that's easy to halve.)

Joedy L. Armstrong of Phoenix was a finalist in the 1981 Movable Feast contest with this.

▼▼▼▼▼▼▼▼▼▼▼▼▼▼▼▼▼▼▼▼▼

**6 to 8 pounds beef brisket (or
  2 small briskets)**
8 cups water
**2 medium yellow onions,
  peeled and quartered**
1 teaspoon salt
**2 teaspoons whole pickling
  spice**
12 whole peppercorns
3 whole cloves
1 bay leaf

GLAZE:
1/2 cup water
1/2 cup dark molasses
**1 teaspoon whole pickling
  spice**
2 teaspoons cider vinegar
**Mustard sauce (*recipe
  follows*)**

Place brisket, water, onions, salt, 2 teaspoons pickling spice, peppercorns, cloves and bay leaf in a large pot. Bring to a boil, cover and simmer about 4 hours, or until meat is fork tender. Remove from heat and let meat cool in pot. Remove from pot and wrap tightly in foil. Refrigerate overnight. In the morning, trim all fat off meat.

Make glaze. Combine water, molasses, 1 teaspoon whole pickling spice and vinegar in a small saucepan. Bring to a boil, then simmer uncovered for 5 minutes. Brush glaze onto both sides of meat.

Preheat broiler. Place glazed meat under the broiler for about 4 to 5 minutes. Remove meat and brush with glaze again.

To serve, slice brisket thinly and serve with mustard sauce. Makes 8 to 12 servings.

MUSTARD SAUCE:
1/2 cup mayonnaise
1/4 cup dark molasses

2 tablespoons prepared
  mustard
2 teaspoons horseradish

Blend all ingredients together in a small bowl. Chill until ready
to serve.

Chicken In Parchment

Susan Nelson

Double this recipe for an easy, nutritious dinner for four. If you
don't have parchment paper (available in gourmet markets), use
aluminum foil to make the packets. The pieces can be coated with
nonstick cooking spray before you put the chicken and vegetables
in place. Susan Nelson was a finalist in the 1984 cookoff that
featured—what else?—Healthy Appetites. This recipe really
fits the bill.

▼▼▼▼▼▼▼▼▼▼▼▼▼▼▼▼▼▼▼▼▼

Margarine or nonstick
  cooking spray
2 chicken breasts, boned and
  skinned
2 tablespoons diced tomato
  (2 slices)
2 mushrooms, diced

2 three-inch pieces green
  onion, diced
Pinch salt
Pinch pepper
1/4 teaspoon lemon juice
1 teaspoon white wine
1/4 teaspoon fines herbes

Cut 12″ piece of parchment paper or foil and fold in half. Cut into
half circle, starting from one edge and arcing to top and back down
to other edge. Coat one side with margarine or cooking spray.

Pound thick end of chicken breast so that breast is of uniform
thickness. Place on buttered side of parchment. Lightly sprinkle
with salt, pepper and fines herbes. Place vegetables on chicken.
Sprinkle with wine and lemon juice. Fold top half of parchment over
chicken so that cut edges meet.

Starting at one edge of parchment, make two small folds and continue making small folds around edge, holding previous fold until
the next one is made. Place parchment package on cookie sheet and
bake at 350° for 10 minutes. To serve, cut parchment open with
scissors and slide contents and juices onto plate. Makes 2 servings.

Panhellenic Western Casserole

Peggy Jordan

Perfect for a Southwestern brunch, this variation of the chili relleno casserole includes white bread for a souffle-like texture. Make it the night before and serve Panhellenic Western Casserole the next morning with fresh fruit. Peggy Jordan of Tempe was a finalist in 1982 with this. A native of Fort Huachuca, she said that her grandmother in Atlanta made a version of this that traveled to Arizona with her mother in the 1920s, when she arrived as a bride at Fort Apache. Jordan returned to The Ranch as a finalist in 1986, with another recipe of her grandmother's. (See Nana's Onions in Wine Sauce, page 73.)

▼▼▼▼▼▼▼▼▼▼▼▼▼▼▼▼▼▼▼▼

4 slices firm white bread	**6 eggs, beaten**
Butter or margarine	**2 cups milk**
2 cups sharp Cheddar cheese, grated	**1 teaspoon salt**
	1/4 teaspoon garlic powder
2 cups Monterey Jack cheese, grated	**1 teaspoon paprika**
	1 teaspoon oregano leaves
1 can (3 1/2 or 4 ounces) chopped green chilies	**1/2 teaspoon pepper**
	1/4 teaspoon dry mustard

Trim and butter 4 slices of bread on one side. Arrange in 9″ by 13″ ovenproof dish coated with nonstick cooking spray. Sprinkle with Cheddar and Jack cheeses, then with green chilies. Beat eggs with remaining ingredients; pour over bread. Cover and chill at least 4 hours, or overnight. Bake in preheated 325° oven for 50 minutes. Makes 6 to 8 servings.

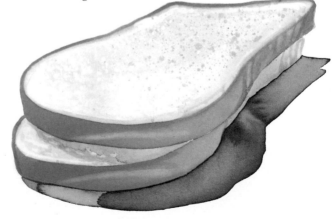

Chicken Encanto

Mary Chard

Mary Haire Chard was inspired to create this recipe after she had
flank steak stuffed with green chilies and cheese, a Phoenix favorite
still sold ready-to-grill by the neighborhood butcher close to Encanto Park. The Tempe native named this dish for the Phoenix street
where she lived when she invented the dish.

When it took the prize in the Neuvo Arizona category of the 1982
Taste of Arizona contest, Chard noted that it was perfect for entertaining because it was easy to serve to a crowd; it could also be
made ahead, frozen and reheated, eliminating last-minute preparation. This recipe is simple to halve.

▼▼▼▼▼▼▼▼▼▼▼▼▼▼▼▼▼▼▼▼

8 whole chicken breasts, skinned, boned and cut in half	**4 tablespoons butter, softened**
3/4 cup chopped green onions	**Salt**
	Flour
1 1/4 cups (10 ounces) chopped green chilies	**4 eggs, beaten**
	2 cups dry bread crumbs
1/2 pound Monterey Jack cheese, grated	**Oil for deep frying**
	Mustard Mornay (*recipe follows*)

In a medium bowl, combine onions, green chilies, cheese and butter. Place mixture on a sheet of waxed paper placed on a plate or
flat surface and pat into a 4″ by 8″ rectangle. Chill.

Place each half chicken breast between 2 pieces of wax paper.
Pound with the flat side of a wooden mallet until ⅛″ thick. Peel off
the paper and lightly sprinkle the chicken with salt.

Cut chilled onion-cheese mixture in half lengthwise, making two
2″ by 8″ strips. Cut each strip into eight 1″ by 2″ pieces. Place a piece
of the onion-cheese mixture at the end of one of the chicken cutlets.
Roll in jellyroll fashion, carefully tucking in the sides to encase the
filling. Press to seal well. Dust with flour; dip in beaten eggs and
roll in bread crumbs. Repeat with remaining chicken cutlets. Chill
1 hour.

In a deep fat fryer or skillet, heat cooking oil to 375°. Cook
breasts, a few at a time, for about 5 minutes, or until golden. May
be served or frozen at this point. If frozen, thaw and reheat in 350°
oven for 30 minutes, or until fat sizzles from chicken. Serve with
mustard Mornay. Makes 16 servings.

MUSTARD MORNAY:

1/4 cup chopped green onions	1/2 cup half-and-half
1/4 cup butter	1/2 tablespoon salt
1/4 cup flour	White pepper to taste
1 1/2 cups chicken stock	1 cup grated Jarlsberg cheese
2 egg yolks	4 teaspoons Dijon mustard

In a medium saucepan, sauté onions in butter. Add flour and sauté 1 minute. Pour in chicken stock and cook, stirring constantly, until thickened. May be prepared to this point one day ahead and refrigerated, covered.

In a small bowl, beat egg yolks with half-and-half. Add a little of the hot mixture to the eggs, stirring well. Add eggs back to the hot mixture. Cook, stirring constantly, until thick. Do not boil. Add seasonings, cheese and mustard, stirring until cheese is melted. Serve hot. May be kept warm in a crock pot on low setting up to 2 hours before serving. Thin, if necessary, with additional half-and-half.

Cornish Picnic Pasties

Sandra L. Shrock

A cold-water pastry envelops the filling of this traditional lunch for miners, who carried them in lunch pails to work in Arizona copper mines as well as everywhere else the Cornish migrated. Sandra L. Schrock, Tempe, sent in this recipe for the 1981 Movable Feast contest. Try serving them with the Mustard Sauce that accompanies Spiced Cold Corn Beef Brisket (page 78).

Pastry for 2-crust pie is also required (your favorite recipe, or use the one for French Picnic Pie on page 89).

▼▼▼▼▼▼▼▼▼▼▼▼▼▼▼▼▼▼▼▼▼

FILLING:

1 1/2 cups peeled and thinly sliced potatoes	2 tablespoons chopped onion
	3/4 pound ground beef
1 small turnip, quartered and thinly sliced	1 tablespoon dried parsley
	1 1/2 teaspoons salt
1/2 cup coarsely chopped carrot	1/2 teaspoon pepper
	2 tablespoons margarine
	1 egg, beaten

Prepare standard pastry for 2-crust pie. Form dough into 6 balls; cover and refrigerate.

In a mixing bowl, combine ground beef, potatoes, turnip, carrot, parsley, onion, salt and pepper. Mix well.

Preheat oven to 425°. To make pasties, roll each ball of dough into 8″ circle. Spread ⅙ of filling on half of each circle. Dot filling with margarine. Moisten edge of each circle. Fold over. Fold edge of bottom crust over top. Seal with fingers.

Make 2 slits in tops of each pasty. Brush top of each with beaten egg. Bake on ungreased cookie sheet 30 minutes at 425°. Cool on wire racks.

Wrap each in foil for transportation. Can be prepared the night before and refrigerated. Next day, wrap in foil and head for picnic. For serving you may want to cut pasties in half and have some mustard sauce handy. Makes 6 servings.

Tortilla Quiche

Peggy Milholland

First you get a tortilla as big as a pizza pan. (In southern Arizona, this is easy to procure. In other areas, you may have to fudge a bit and overlap smaller ones.) Then you line a pie plate with said tortilla. Presto — it's a quiche crust. Very pretty, and what could be easier? Peggy Milholland of Scottsdale submitted this for the 1987 Zest of the Southwest contest. It's a variation of the ever-popular green chili-and-cheese pie that everyone in Phoenix makes sooner or later. All such dishes are closely related to the chili relleno.

▼▼▼▼▼▼▼▼▼▼▼▼▼▼▼▼▼▼▼

1 (12-inch) flour tortilla	1 can (3 1/2 or 4 ounces)
1 1/2 cups grated jack	chopped green chilies
cheese	3 eggs
1 cup grated sharp Cheddar	1 cup sour cream
cheese	1/4 teaspoon salt
	1/8 teaspoon cumin

Preheat oven to 350°. Place tortilla in bottom of a lightly greased, 10″ pie plate. Sprinkle jack cheese and half of Cheddar cheese over tortilla. Sprinkle chilies over cheese. Beat eggs, sour cream, salt and cumin. Pour over chilies and top with the rest of the Cheddar cheese. Bake for 45 minutes at 350°. Let sit 10 minutes before cutting. Makes 6 servings.

Blue Corn Tamale Pie with Butterfly Guaymas Shrimp and Goat Cheese

Nancy Gerczynski

This recipe almost made Nancy Gerczynski a two-time grand prize winner. The Phoenix resident's creative No-Title Turkey (page 94) won the big money in 1984, and the 1987 judges loved this updated hometown favorite in the Zest of the Southwest contest. It topped the entrées category and was a close tie for the grand prize. A trip to a gourmet market will supply you with blue cornmeal and goat cheese. If you want to make a less expensive version, substitute chicken chunks for the jumbo shrimp and, yes, plain old yellow or white cornmeal for the trendier blue.

▼▼▼▼▼▼▼▼▼▼▼▼▼▼▼▼▼▼▼▼

1 cup ground blue cornmeal
1/2 cup masa harina
2 teaspoons salt, divided
4 teaspoons melted butter
3/4 cup water
1 pound jumbo Guaymas
** shrimp (raw, shelled,**
** cleaned and butterflied)**
1 teaspoon ancho chilie
** flakes**
1/2 teaspoon lemon zest
1 teaspoon ground black
** pepper, divided**
1 teaspoon lemon juice
1 tablespoon olive oil

1 clove garlic, minced
6 ounces fresh goat cheese
4 ounces cream cheese
1/4 cup milk
3 egg whites
1 Serrano chilie, seeded and
** finely minced**
2 Anaheim chilies, roasted,
** peeled, seeded and chopped**
2/3 cup corn (cut from cob
** or defrosted)**
2 tablespoons freshly grated
** Parmesan cheese**
Cilantro leaves for garnish
Lemon slices

Preheat oven to 375°. In a medium mixing bowl, combine blue cornmeal, masa harina and ½ teaspoon salt. Cut in melted butter until blended well. Slowly add water, stirring until a ball is formed. With dry hands, form ball, kneading lightly to incorporate ingredients. Flatten slightly, and let rest, covered, for 10 minutes. Press carefully into 9" diameter deep pie pan. Mixture should be ½" thick. Cover and refrigerate for 30 minutes before filling.

Toss shrimp with chili flakes, lemon zest, ½ teaspoon salt, ½ teaspoon pepper, lemon juice, oil and garlic. Refrigerate in a tightly covered non-metal bowl for 1 hour.

In a large non-stick skillet, quickly sauté shrimp over medium-high heat until shrimp are barely pink and just opaque. Remove from heat and set aside. In blender or food processor, thoroughly mix goat cheese, cream cheese, milk, egg whites, remaining 1 teaspoon salt and remaining ½ teaspoon pepper until smooth.

Drain any accumulated juices from shrimp into cheese mixture, and blend. Toss Serrano and Anaheim chilies with shrimp. Mix corn into shrimp mixture and carefully fill pie shell with shrimp. Pour cheese mixture over shrimp.

Dust with 2 tablespoons Parmesan cheese and bake at 375° until filling is set and top is just lightly browned, about 25 to 30 minutes.

Let set for 15 minutes at room temperature before serving. Garnish with cilantro leaves and lemon slices. Makes 4 to 6 servings.

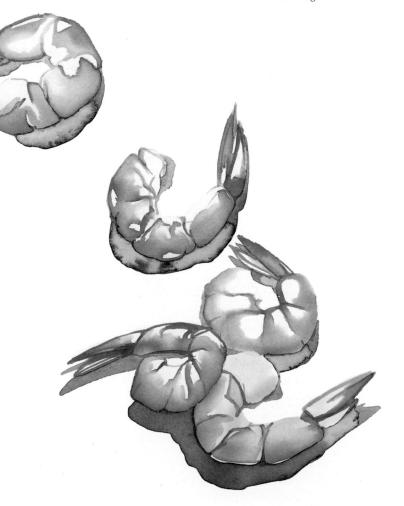

Green Corn Tamales

Esperanza Marsh

Even newcomers to Arizona who know a lot about Mexican food are puzzled the first time a waitress asks them if they want a green or red tamale. Once they've ordered their first green one, however, they're hooked — the legislature should declare the Green Corn Tamale our official state food. Restaurants today serve them year round, but green tamales were originally a summer specialty, made only when fresh white corn was available. Mesa's Esperanza Marsh submitted this recipe (under the name Green Chili Tamales) to the 1982 Taste of Arizona contest. It's the real thing.

▼▼▼▼▼▼▼▼▼▼▼▼▼▼▼▼▼▼▼

12 ears of white corn with husks	**1 cup Monterey Jack cheese**
3/4 cup vegetable shortening	**3 cups Cheddar cheese**
	3 cans (3 1/2 or 4 ounces each) chopped green chilies
2 teaspoons salt	
1 teaspoon sugar	**1 1/2 cups hot water**

Carefully remove husks from cobs; rinse husks and set aside. With a sharp knife, cut kernels from cobs. Mash corn until it is the consistency of oatmeal to make the *masa* for the tamales. Use a food processor for the best results.

Place masa in a large bowl and thoroughly blend in shortening, salt and sugar. Then add cheeses and mix together.

Place husk on a flat surface and spread about 2 heaping tablespoons of masa on the widest side. Place 3 teaspoons of green chilies in the middle and roll husks, folding the opposite end of husk to form tamale. Continue doing this until you've used all the masa.

Line the bottom of a Dutch oven with the extra husks and add 1½ cups of hot water. Stand tamales with open end up; cover and let boil for 3 to 4 minutes at high temperature. Decrease heat to low and cook for 45 minutes. Tamales are done when masa does not stick to the husk. Makes 2 or 3 dozen.

Asado A La Peruana
(Peruvian Pot Roast)

Adriana Sofia Richard

Judges in the 1988 Easy Entertaining recipe contest almost gave the category prize to this dish, which they said pairs a homey fork-tender pot roast with the exotic taste of cuminseed. Scottsdale's Adriana Sofia Richard, born in Lima, Peru, was the finalist, and she advised those who would make this to serve it with mashed potatoes and the wonderful gravy the roast makes while cooking.

▼▼▼▼▼▼▼▼▼▼▼▼▼▼▼▼▼▼▼▼

10 to 12 cloves fresh garlic
1 teaspoon cuminseeds
2 teaspoons salt, divided
**2 teaspoons black pepper,
  divided**
**1 boneless round tip roast
  (4 to 4 1/2 pounds)**
**1/4 cup vegetable oil for
  browning roast**

**1 can (15 ounces) tomato
  sauce**
**1 to 1 1/2 cups blush or red
  wine**
Water
**1 medium onion, chopped in
  1 1/2" slices**
**Cornstarch mixed with water,
  as needed**

Mash fresh garlic. Mix garlic well with cuminseeds and 1 teaspoon each of salt and pepper to make a paste (about 1½ tablespoons).

With a knife, cut 1"-deep slices around roast (slices should be approximately 1½" apart). Stuff the slices with the garlic mixture.

In a pot big enough to accommodate the roast, with a tight-fitting lid, heat the oil. Add the roast and brown it well on all sides. When the roast is browned, pour in the tomato sauce and wine and enough water to bring the liquid level to the middle of the roast. Add onion with 1 teaspoon salt and 1 teaspoon pepper. Stir well, without removing the roast from the pan.

Cover pan and bring to a boil. Lower heat and simmer over low heat, turning the roast every 15 to 20 minutes. When the meat is done, about 2 hours, remove it from the pot.

Add cornstarch mixed with water to gravy, as needed, to thicken. Serve sliced roast with gravy and mashed potatoes. Makes 6 servings.

Red Snapper Fiesta

Diane Howells

Diane Howells' recipe for the 1984 Healthy Appetites contest gets a flavor boost from the vegetables. Perhaps best of all, it's a snap to put together and shove in the microwave. The amount of cheese can be halved, if you wish, and you can cut up a few fresh mushrooms to substitute for the canned ones.

▼▼▼▼▼▼▼▼▼▼▼▼▼▼▼▼▼▼▼▼

1 pound (about 4 fillets) red snapper
3/4 cup chopped onion
3/4 cup chopped tomato
1/4 cup chopped green pepper

1 can (4 ounces) mushroom pieces, drained
Salt and pepper
1 to 2 tablespoons butter or margarine
1 cup Cheddar cheese, shredded

Check fillets for bones, and remove any you find. Place snapper in a 10″ by 10″ microwave-safe baking dish that has been coated with nonstick cooking spray. Sprinkle with salt and pepper. Sprinkle onion, tomato, green pepper and mushrooms on top of fillets. Dot with butter.

Cook, covered, in microwave oven at full power for 3 minutes. Turn dish halfway and cook another 3 minutes. Turn dish halfway and cook another 3 minutes or until fish flakes when tested with fork. Sprinkle cheese over fish. Cook for 2 more minutes or until cheese has melted. Makes 4 servings.

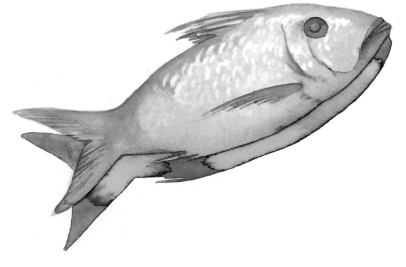

French Picnic Pie

Teresa Stavros

Another thoughtful way with ground turkey. Teresa Stavros of Phoenix was our first-ever main dish winner in the 1981 Movable Feast contest. This recipe makes use of an underutilized herb: parsley. Too often, its role is to just sit on the sidelines and be green. Minced into a main mixture, in a generous amount like this, it adds an extra flavor zing.

▼▼▼▼▼▼▼▼▼▼▼▼▼▼▼▼▼▼▼

Egg pastry (*recipe below*)	**1/2 cup soft bread crumbs**
2 tablespoons butter	**1/4 cup parsley, chopped fine**
1 small onion, chopped	**1 egg, slightly beaten**
2 cloves garlic, minced	**1/2 teaspoon salt**
1/2 cup dry white wine	**1/2 teaspoon thyme**
1 pound ground turkey or	**1/2 teaspoon dry mustard**
veal	**1/4 teaspoon allspice**
1/2 pound ground ham	**1/8 teaspoon white pepper**

In a saucepan or small skillet, sauté onion in butter until clear, but not brown. In a large bowl, mix all the other ingredients in order; add onions and butter to the mixture. Blend with large spoon. Mixture will resemble a meat loaf before it is cooked.

Preheat oven to 375°. Line a 9″ pie pan with half the rolled-out pastry. Pour filling into crust. Arrange second layer of pastry over top. Bake at 375° on the lowest oven rack 40 to 50 minutes. Serve warm or cold. Makes 6 to 8 servings.

EGG PASTRY:

2 cups flour	**1/4 cup shortening**
1/2 teaspoon salt	**1 egg yolk, plus enough water**
1/4 cup butter	**to make 1/3 cup**

Sift together the flour and salt. Cut in the butter and shortening with a pastry blender or fork until pieces are the size of small peas. Add egg yolk and water mixture. Gently mix with fork until all is moistened. Gather up with fingers; form into ball. Let stand several minutes. Divide dough in half. Form into two balls. Flatten each slightly and roll on lightly floured pastry cloth.

Indian Tacos

Judy Greer

"Do you have a recipe for Indian Tacos?" was a question I heard a lot as a food editor. Yes, I did, and we printed it regularly; cookbooks outside the state just don't include this Arizona specialty. I've been lucky enough to consume this meal-in-itself in the cafe in Supai at the bottom of the Grand Canyon, at the visitor's center on the Gila River Indian Reservation (a must-stop anytime we head south on I-10), at Indian festivals and at the Arizona State Fair. I've always wondered which booth at the state fair serves the best ones, but I can't persuade myself to buy them anywhere but my favorite place, which serves the same great mounded meal year after year. (Traditional dessert variation: drizzle fry bread with honey.) This recipe came from Judy Greer of Mesa to our 1982 Taste of Arizona contest.

▼▼▼▼▼▼▼▼▼▼▼▼▼▼▼▼▼▼▼▼

FRY BREAD:
2 cups flour
1/2 cup dry milk powder
1 tablespoon baking powder
1/2 teaspoon salt
2 tablespoons lard or
 shortening
3/4 cup water
Shortening for deep frying

FILLINGS:
3 cups heated refried beans
Shredded lettuce
Chopped tomato
Chopped green onion
Grated cheese
Sliced or mashed avocado
 (optional)
Sour cream and taco sauce
 (optional)

To make fry bread, combine dry ingredients and lard in a mixing bowl; mix well with fingers. Stir in water with a fork. Knead until smooth. Divide into 6 equal parts. Roll into 8" circles ¼" thick. Fry in hot shortening (365°) until brown on one side; turn with tongs and brown other side. Drain and place between paper towels.

Spread each piece of fry bread with ½ cup refried beans. Add lettuce, tomato, green onion, cheese, avocado, sour cream and taco sauce. Makes 6 servings.

Jerky Dumplings

William D. Miller

William D. Miller of Chandler won high marks for originality with this recipe when he was a finalist in the 1987 Zest of the Southwest contest. The colorful dumplings are perfect for a Sunday supper, accompanied by a green vegetable. When you make this, go to the trouble of tracking down the good kind of jerky, made from whole strips of meat (not chopped and formed, please). The aroma of these dumplings cooking will haunt your hungry moments for months to come.

▼▼▼▼▼▼▼▼▼▼▼▼▼▼▼▼▼▼▼▼▼

1 clove garlic
4 ounces (about 4 to 6 sticks) hot peppered beef jerky
12 cups beef stock (canned or homemade)
1 1/2 cups cornmeal
2 1/2 cups flour
1 teaspoon salt
1 1/2 tablespoons baking powder

2 tablespoons (1/2 large) fresh Anaheim chilie pepper, finely chopped
1/2 cup (1/2 large) green bell pepper, finely chopped
1/3 cup (1/3 large) red bell pepper, finely chopped
1/2 cup butter, melted and cooled
1 cup water
Chopped parsley for garnish

Combine garlic, jerky and beef stock in an 8-quart stock pan. Bring to a boil and simmer 2 hours. Remove jerky and shred finely. (Chop any long shreds into smaller pieces with a knife, or snip with kitchen shears.)

Combine shredded jerky with cornmeal, flour, salt, baking powder, chilies and green and red peppers. Mix well. Add butter and water. Mix until batter is stiff.

Bring beef stock to boil and drop 1 tablespoon of batter at a time into the boiling stock. (If stock has reduced, cook dumplings in two batches.) Reduce heat to medium and cook, covered, 20 to 25 minutes. Serve in bowls with parsley garnish. Makes 32 dumplings, about 8 servings.

Buzzard's Breath Revenge Chili

Pappy Beier

Thirty-year Arizona resident Pappy Beier of Casa Grande entered the 1987 Zest of the Southwest cookoff at the urging of his wife Laurie. He developed this chili by trial-and-error over a period of five years. He got the taste just right after he switched to better cuts of meat, he said.

▼▼▼▼▼▼▼▼▼▼▼▼▼▼▼▼▼▼▼▼▼

3 pounds boneless beef chuck
3 pounds boneless pork roast
2 large green bell peppers, coarsely chopped
4 celery stalks, coarsely chopped
2 large onions, diced
4 garlic cloves, diced
2 tablespoons vegetable oil
2 teaspoons salt, or to taste
2 teaspoons ground cumin

2 teaspoons Mexican oregano
6 to 8 tablespoons hot red chili powder
4 to 5 tablespoons mild red chili powder
2 cans (6 ounces each) tomato paste
2 cans (12 ounces each) beer
3 to 4 cups of water
1 package (2 ounces) slivered almonds

Trim beef and pork of all fat and gristle. Cook fat slowly in a heavy 8-quart pot over medium heat. Discard crisp pieces of fat. Cut beef and pork into ½" cubes. Brown meat, a third at a time, in hot fat over high heat, removing cubes with slotted spoon as they brown.

Reduce heat to medium. Add green bell peppers, celery, onions and garlic, stirring often; cook for about 5 minutes. Add oil if needed to keep vegetables from sticking. Stir in remaining ingredients (except almonds) and browned beef. Heat to boiling over high heat, then reduce heat to low and let simmer for 2 hours, or until meat is tender.

Add the slivered almonds after 1½ hours. If you want the chili more thickened, combine ¼ cup each cornstarch and water and stir the mixture into the chili. Cook until bubbly. If chili is too spicy, dilute with 2 teaspoons of vinegar and cook another 10 minutes. Makes 8 to 12 large servings.

Chinle Lamb

Judy Wood

This was one of the entries in the Indian category of the 1982 Taste of Arizona contest. I'm not sure how authentic Gilbert resident Judy Woods' recipe is, but I do know how delicious it is. Plus it's easy to make and serve. The pine nut sauce is excellent with the chops, on other grilled meats, or in any way you want to use it. In the past, it's been hard to find good pine nuts, which go rancid if they sit unrefrigerated too long. The best place to buy them is in a busy Italian deli, or from the nut shops set up in some malls.

▼▼▼▼▼▼▼▼▼▼▼▼▼▼▼▼▼▼▼▼▼▼

4 lean shoulder lamb chops, about 1-inch thick
SAUCE:
1/2 cup pine nuts (about 3 ounces; also called piñons or pignolia)
3 large garlic cloves, peeled and minced

2 dried hot red chilies, about 1 inch long, stemmed, seeded and chopped
3/4 cup olive oil
1 can (6 ounces) tomato paste
1/2 teaspoon salt
2 tablespoons distilled white vinegar
1 teaspoon sugar

In a small, ungreased skillet, place the pine nuts; toast, stirring frequently over moderate heat for 5 minutes.

In a blender or food processor, place ¼ cup of the toasted pine nuts. Add remaining sauce ingredients. Blend or process to a smooth paste.

Place each lamb chop on a barbecue grill over a bed of hot coals. Brush each chop with 1 tablespoon of the sauce. Broil 4 to 6 minutes; turn chops over and coat each with another tablespoon of the sauce. Broil until chops are slightly pink in center. Serve on heated platter garnished with remaining pine nuts and parsley. Warm remaining sauce and serve on the side. Makes 4 servings.

No-Title Turkey

Nancy Gerczynski

From the minute the dish entered the judges' sequestered chambers, it led the pack; all five chefs gave it an outstanding rating. Ground turkey was just beginning to be widely available in supermarkets when this recipe was published. In terms of reader response, it became one of the most successful winners we ever had. (*Bonus:* No extra dishes to wash: this dish is made and served in one skillet.)

▼▼▼▼▼▼▼▼▼▼▼▼▼▼▼▼▼▼▼▼▼

3 cups fresh spinach,
  coarsely chopped
1 large onion, chopped
2 teaspoons margarine
1 cup fresh mushrooms,
  sliced
1 clove garlic, minced
1 teaspoon olive oil
1 1/2 pounds ground turkey
1 clove garlic, mashed
1/4 teaspoon salt
2 cups plain yogurt

1 cup Monterey Jack cheese,
  cubed
1/2 cup fresh grated
  Parmesan cheese
2 large eggs
1/4 teaspoon ground black
  pepper
1/2 teaspoon salt
Pinch of fresh, grated
  nutmeg
3 tablespoons fresh, grated
  Parmesan cheese
Paprika

Rinse spinach well, leaving water on leaves. In skillet, using collapsible steamer, steam spinach until just wilted. Remove steamer with spinach still in it, cover and set aside. Empty water from skillet; wipe dry.

Over medium heat, sauté chopped onion in margarine until soft but not browned. Add mushrooms and minced garlic and sauté until mushrooms are soft and dark. Remove mixture from pan and set aside with spinach, keeping covered.

Add olive oil to skillet. Over medium-high heat, sauté ground turkey and mashed garlic in olive oil. Sauté until turkey is no longer pink, crumbling with spoon while cooking. Discard garlic. Remove turkey from heat. Add ¼ teaspoon salt.

Drain juices from turkey and reserve. Pour juices, yogurt, Monterey Jack cheese and ½ cup Parmesan cheese into blender. Blend until smooth. Then blend in eggs. Spread reserved spinach and mushroom mixture over turkey. Sprinkle with nutmeg, ½ teaspoon salt and pepper. Pour cheese-egg mixture over all and top with remaining 3 tablespoons Parmesan cheese. Bake in preheated 350° oven for 30 to 35 minutes, until topping is set and slightly browned. Sprinkle with paprika and let stand for 10 minutes before serving. Makes 4 to 6 servings.

Chilaquiles

Silvia P. Sandersius

Chilaquiles and bread pudding share a similar origin. Both were no doubt invented to use up stale bread products. This homey Mexican dish is usually served for breakfast with an egg on top; if you're lucky, you may find a restaurant that serves chilaquiles. This version, from Silvia P. Sandersius of Phoenix, is heartier. It was submitted to the 1987 Zest of the Southwest contest in the Side Dishes category, but I think it makes a fine main dish.

▼▼▼▼▼▼▼▼▼▼▼▼▼▼▼▼▼▼▼▼

1 whole chicken, 2 1/2 to 3 pounds
Water to cover
Salt and pepper
4 fresh jalapeño peppers, seeded
1 can (6 ounces) tomato sauce
3 cups chicken broth
2 medium onions, 1 diced, 1 sliced
2 dozen corn tortillas
Oil for frying
16 ounces sour cream
3 cups shredded mozzarella cheese

In a large pot, cover chicken with water and bring to a boil. Cover and reduce heat. When chicken is tender, remove and allow to cool. Reserve 3 cups chicken broth.

When chicken is cool, remove skin and shred the meat. Season to taste with salt and pepper. In blender, mix jalapeños and tomato sauce. In a saucepan, add blended sauce to chicken broth and diced onion. Simmer 15 to 20 minutes.

With scissors, cut tortillas into quarters; cut each quarter in half. Heat oil for frying in a skillet. Lightly brown the cut tortillas in hot oil. Drain on paper towels.

Mix chicken and tortillas in a 10″ by 13″ ovenproof dish. Add the sauce; mix. Evenly add sour cream by spoonfuls. Spread cheese over top. Put sliced onion over cheese. Heat in oven at 300° for about 20 minutes, or until cheese is melted. Makes 8 to 10 servings.

Southwestern Sweet and Sour Squealer

Val Craig

A 1987 finalist, Val Craig of Phoenix, developed this recipe using a new cut of boneless pork called the sirloin—chops cut from the end of the loin. He rolled them around sticks of flavored masa harina, which is traditionally used as a tamale filling, and sauced the pork rolls with a combination of chicken stock, honey, lime juice, garlic, jalapeño and cilantro. The chili oil is a special weapon of Szechwan cooks. Fire-eaters will find plenty of other uses for this ingredient. (For one, see the recipe for Vietnamese Chicken Salad, page 39.)

▼▼▼▼▼▼▼▼▼▼▼▼▼▼▼▼▼▼▼▼

2 boneless pork sirloin steaks, 1 pound each (chop cut from end of pork loin)	**1/2 cup grated jack cheese**
	1 cup masa harina (instant)
1 tablespoon chili oil (available at Oriental markets)	**1 cup plus 1 tablespoon water**
1/4 cup fresh lime juice	**1 cup Southwestern Sweet and Sour Sauce (recipe follows)**
1 red bell pepper	
2 long green Anaheim chilies	**2 tablespoons salad oil**

Cut each steak in half against the grain. Place each steak between 2 sheets of wax paper and flatten with a mallet to ⅛" thickness. Sprinkle with chili oil and lime juice; cover and refrigerate 2 hours.

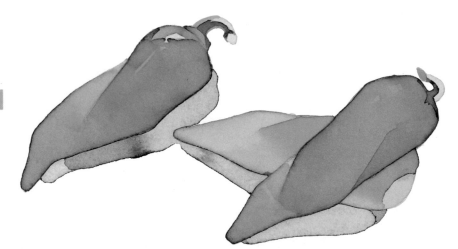

Meanwhile, roast and peel red pepper and green chilies. (For roasting instructions, see recipe for Caldo de Queso y Chile Verde, page 27.) Cut green chilies in half and remove seeds. Cut red pepper in quarters and remove seeds. Mix masa harina with water and shape into four equal sticks and set aside.

Make Southwestern Sweet and Sour Sauce.

Assemble pork rolls: onto each steak place half a green chilie and a red pepper quarter, 1 tablespoon grated cheese, and 1 masa stick. Roll up jelly-roll style and secure with toothpick.

Preheat broiler to 500°. Heat oil in an 8″ iron skillet until very hot. Place pork rolls in ovenproof skillet and brown 1 minute on each side. Place pan on low rack of broiler and broil 6 to 8 minutes, turning frequently. Remove from oven and remove picks.

To serve, place ¼ cup Sweet and Sour Sauce on plate and top with pork roll.

SOUTHWESTERN SWEET AND SOUR SAUCE:
1/2 cup chicken stock
1/4 cup honey
1/4 cup fresh lime juice
2 large cloves garlic
1/2 jalapeño pepper, seeded and minced
1 tablespoon cornstarch
1 tablespoon water
2 tablespoons chopped cilantro

Place all ingredients except cilantro, cornstarch and water in saucepan. Cook over medium heat and simmer for 5 minutes. Mix cornstarch and water and add to sauce. Cook until thickened, 3 to 5 minutes more. Add chopped cilantro. Remove from heat. Makes· 1 cup sauce.

Breast of Chicken with Zucchini, Mushrooms

Madeline Keller

A plus here: no skillet to wash or broiler to clean. Chicken and vegetables in aluminum foil packets won the entrée category for Madeline Keller in the 1984 Healthy Appetites contest. The chicken is flavored with Dijon mustard, onion, mushrooms, basil and a sprinkle of Parmesan cheese. Calories are kept low with the use of diet margarine, and the fat content is negligible.

▼▼▼▼▼▼▼▼▼▼▼▼▼▼▼▼▼▼▼▼

1 medium onion, sliced
4 chicken breast halves,
  boned and skinned
Salt and pepper
Dijon mustard
2 medium zucchini or yellow
  squash, sliced 1/4″ thick
1/2 pound mushrooms,
  sliced

3 tablespoons diet
  margarine
3/4 teaspoon dried basil
1/8 teaspoon garlic powder
1/8 teaspoon paprika
1 tablespoon grated
  Parmesan cheese

Tear off four 12″ by 18″ lengths of heavy-duty aluminum foil. Place onion slices in center of lower half of each length of foil. With rolling pin, flatten chicken breasts to ¼″ thick. Place chicken breasts on top of onion slices. Season with salt and pepper and spread lightly with mustard. Top with zucchini and mushrooms. Season vegetables with salt and pepper. Dot with margarine. Sprinkle with basil, garlic powder and paprika.

Fold upper edge of foil over ingredients to meet bottom edge. Turn up edges to form ½″ fold. Smooth fold, double over again and press very tightly to seal, allowing a little extra room for heat circulation and expansion. Follow same directions for folding each end. Place foil packets in single layer on large cookie sheet. Bake at 450° for 25 minutes or until chicken is done.

To serve, cut an X in top of foil packets. Fold foil back. Top each serving with ¾ teaspoon Parmesan cheese. Makes 4 servings.

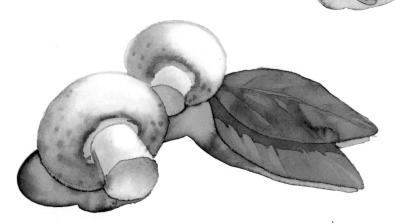

Cheesy Seafood Lasagna Rolls

Patricia Lapiezo

Here's another creation of the talented sisters, Pat Lapezio and Peggy Milholland; this one brought Pat once again from La Mesa, California, to compete in the 1988 Easy Entertaining contest. A colorful, impressive entrée, one that can be made ahead of time, it works well using the less-costly crab substitutes that are now so popular.

▼▼▼▼▼▼▼▼▼▼▼▼▼▼▼▼▼▼▼▼▼

15 ounces ricotta cheese
4 ounces (1 cup) shredded
  mozzarella cheese
1/4 cup grated Parmesan
  cheese
1 package (10 1/2 ounces)
  chopped frozen spinach,
  thawed and drained
1 pound bay shrimp
1 pound crab meat, shredded
Salt and pepper to taste
12 lasagna noodles (8
  ounces) cooked according
  to package directions

SAUCE:
4 tablespoons butter
4 tablespoons flour
3 cups half-and-half
1/3 cup chopped onion
1/4 cup sherry
1 teaspoon chopped dried
  basil
1 teaspoon chopped dried
  oregano
Salt to taste
Pepper to taste

In a medium bowl, mix the cheeses, spinach, shrimp and crab together. Season with salt and pepper. Lay noodles out on a work surface. Spread an even layer of filling on each and roll up. Place the rolls in a 9″ by 11″ baking pan coated with cooking spray. (At this point, you may refrigerate for convenience. Just wait to pour the sauce over until right before baking and add an extra 10 minutes to the cooking time.)

To prepare sauce, melt butter in a saucepan. Whisk in flour. Add the remaining ingredients and cook over medium-high heat, stirring often, until reduced and slightly thickened.

Pour sauce over the lasagna rolls, and bake at 350° for 20 to 25 minutes. Makes 12 servings.

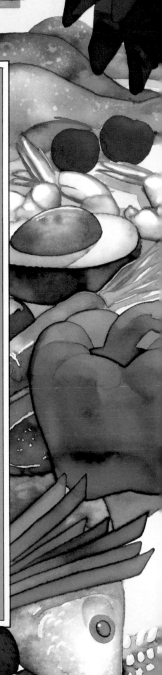

DESSERTS

When I first became a food editor, I quickly realized there was one type of recipe valued above all others: those for desserts. Recipes abound, but people always crave another.

Why do dessert recipes proliferate? One reason is because dessert ingredients can be pricey, so people want guidelines in combining these lush favorites like chocolate, cream, raspberries...the list could go on forever. Another reason is the everlasting popularity of desserts in restaurants — After a slimming "spa cuisine" entrée, the dessert cart is more appreciated than ever. Creative cooks run home to recreate that outstanding finale to a meal, eager to serve it to appreciative guests. Too, some people are dessert hobbyists and will happily spend a Sunday concocting an outrageously rich and wonderful dessert.

This is the longest chapter because we always had more dessert entries in contests than in any other type of category. And, we even had one whole contest devoted to these treats: in 1983, the theme was Just Desserts. We were not surprised when we were deluged with recipes; it was one of our most popular competitions.

As in the other chapters, you will find a wide range of recipes here: luscious cheesecakes; an eggless and milkless-cake; Coffee Nut Tortoni; a simple but delicous Chocolate Applesauce Cake. One of the novelty recipes I couldn't resist including was requested a couple of times by readers in later years: Potato Chip Cookies.

Peachy Tortillas

Jane Walsh

Desserts that could be made at the last minute comprised one entire category in the 1982 Just Desserts recipe contest. The resulting recipes were easy but so appealing. This is one of them, from Jane Walsh. You can make it with peaches, or substitute apples.

The Sonoran signature bread, flour tortillas big enough to cover a small-size pizza pan, is used here. Tortilla-makers pride themselves on the thinness of their tortillas, which gives a crispy delicacy to cheese crisps, chimichangas and other simple dishes such as this one.

▼▼▼▼▼▼▼▼▼▼▼▼▼▼▼▼▼▼▼▼▼

2 large peaches (or apples)
4 large flour tortillas
   (approximately 10″ in
   diameter)

2 tablespoons butter or
   margarine
Cinnamon and sugar, to
   taste

Peel peaches and slice thinly. Arrange slices in a row near center of tortilla. Fold tortilla over peach slices. Repeat until you have filled all four tortillas.

In a large skillet, over medium heat, melt butter or margarine. Place filled tortillas in skillet and fry 4 to 5 minutes until golden-brown, turning once.

Remove from skillet, sprinkle with cinnamon and sugar and serve. Makes 4 servings.

Tarte Au Citron (Lemon Pecan Tart)

Margaret Rhodes

Here's another winning recipe from Margaret Rhodes of Prescott. This was the favorite of the judges in the Desert Desserts category of the 1983 Just Desserts recipe contest. The minced pecans in the crust and the whole pecans garnishing the top are perfect counterpoints to the well-balanced filling. This is another recipe for lemon lovers.

▼▼▼▼▼▼▼▼▼▼▼▼▼▼▼▼▼▼▼▼▼▼

CRUST:
2 tablespoons minced pecans
1 cup minus 2 tablespoons
  all-purpose flour
1/2 cup unsalted butter
1/4 cup confectioners' sugar
2 teaspoons fresh lemon
  juice
1/8 teaspoon salt
FILLING:
2/3 cup sugar
2 large eggs

Grated rind of 1 medium
  lemon
3 tablespoons fresh lemon
  juice
2 1/2 tablespoons flour
1/2 teaspoon baking powder
Pinch of salt
GLAZE:
2 tablespoons honey
2 teaspoons lemon juice
GARNISH:
1 cup pecan halves

Place rack in center of oven and preheat oven to 375°. Using mixer or food processor, combine minced pecans, flour, butter, confectioner's sugar, lemon juice and salt until mixture cleans sides of bowl and forms into a ball of dough. Pat evenly onto bottom and sides of fluted tart or quiche pan with removable bottom. Bake at 375° for 18 minutes or until lightly golden.

While crust is baking, prepare filling. Combine sugar, eggs, lemon rind, lemon juice, flour, baking powder and pinch of salt in food processor or mixer bowl until mixture is thick and lemon-colored.

When crust is golden, remove from oven and reduce oven temperature to 350°. Pour filling over hot crust and return to oven for 25 minutes. Remove from oven. Arrange pecan halves in a spiral or spoke design on top.

In a small saucepan, heat honey and lemon juice for glaze. Brush glaze across pecans. Allow tart to cool before removing from pan. Makes 6 to 8 servings.

Nostalgia Pudding

Minnabel Laughlin

In the tradition of all bread puddings, this 1988 finalist recipe provides a good way to use up the remainder of a loaf. Tempe resident Minnabel Laughlin got an old-fashioned flavor in her Nostalgia Pudding by using apricots and almonds. Minnabel suggested adding semisweet chocolate sauce as an option, which we also favor.

▼▼▼▼▼▼▼▼▼▼▼▼▼▼▼▼▼▼▼▼▼

Butter or margarine
10 to 12 slices (1/4″ thick)
**   day-old French bread**
1 can (16 ounces) apricot
**   halves (reserve juice)**
3 cups milk
2 eggs, slightly beaten

3/4 cup sugar
1/4 teaspoon salt
1/2 teaspoon almond extract
1 teaspoon vanilla extract
1/2 cup sliced almonds
Sauce (*recipe follows*)

Butter a 8″ by 8″ by 2″ baking dish. Trim crusts from bread. Cover bottom of the baking dish with half the slices. Drain apricots, reserving juice. Cut each apricot half into 4 slices and place the slices on top of the bread. Top with another layer of bread slices.

Mix together milk, eggs, sugar, salt and extracts. Pour mixture over the bread. Let it soak for at least 1 hour. (Place in refrigerator if soaking longer than 2 hours.)

Spread almonds over all and bake in preheated 350° oven until the center tests done, as for custard, about 30 minutes. Consistency will be souffle-like and is best served warm or at room temperature. Serve with sauce. Makes 9 servings.

SAUCE:
Reserved apricot juice
2 tablespoons sugar

2 tablespoons butter
2 tablespoons brandy

Combine the juice and sugar in a saucepan and cook until reduced slightly, to the consistency of a thin sauce. Remove from heat and stir in butter and brandy. (*Option:* Semisweet chocolate sauce also can be drizzled over for taste and contrast.)

Tropical Curry

Doris F. Brown

Talk about easy...this is about as simple as it gets. Add any other fresh fruit you crave to this basic recipe, submitted by Doris F. Brown to the 1984 Healthy Appetites contest. The curry is the flavor secret, of course, but even without it, the dressing is good (and low in calories) on any kind of fruit combination.

▼▼▼▼▼▼▼▼▼▼▼▼▼▼▼▼▼▼▼

1 cup seedless green grapes
1 cup canned mandarin
   orange sections, drained,
   or 1 cup fresh orange
   segments

DRESSING:
1 cup low-fat yogurt, plain
2 tablespoons honey
1 teaspoon lime juice
1/2 teaspoon curry powder
1/4 cup shredded coconut

Halve grapes and combine with orange sections; chill. In a small bowl, combine yogurt, honey, lime juice and curry powder. Mix yogurt dressing with chilled fruit. Spoon mixture into dessert dishes. Sprinkle with coconut before serving. Makes 4 servings.

Pears 'n Cream

Lee Springer

This warm, homey dessert is from a 1988 finalist, Lee Springer of Glendale. Think of it when fresh pears are in season. (Of course, if you want to try it in winter with canned pears, I won't tell anybody.)

▼▼▼▼▼▼▼▼▼▼▼▼▼▼▼▼▼▼▼▼

1 ounce butter
5 tablespoons brown sugar

4 large pears, unpeeled,
halved and cored
1/2 pint whipping cream

Butter a shallow 9″ baking pan with approximately half the butter. Sprinkle the sugar over the bottom. Place the pears, cut-side down, in the dish. Dot pears with the rest of the butter.

Bake in preheated 375° oven for 30 to 45 minutes, depending upon the degree of ripeness of the pears. Pour cream over the pears, and bake until tender, another 15 to 20 minutes. Serve warm.

Makes 8 servings.

Cafe Mexicana Cheesecake

Patricia Lapiezo

As I mentioned earlier, one year, two sisters were finalists in the dessert category. (It was 1987, and the contest was Zest of the Southwest.) And they both made cheesecakes. This is Patricia Lapezio's recipe, which she brought to the contest from her home in La Mesa, California. Her sister, Peggy Milholland of Scottsdale, mails Mexican coffee to Lapezio from Arizona, and Patricia used the flavor in her creation.

▼▼▼▼▼▼▼▼▼▼▼▼▼▼▼▼▼▼▼▼

CRUST:
1/4 cup chocolate wafer
  crumbs
1/4 cup butter, melted
1 tablespoon sugar
1/4 teaspoon cinnamon
FILLING:
4 packages (8 ounces each)
  cream cheese, softened
1 1/2 cups sugar
4 large eggs

1 cup sour cream
1/4 cup coffee-flavored
  liqueur
1 teaspoon vanilla
1 cup whipping cream
1 cup semisweet chocolate
  chips, melted
1/2 teaspoon cinnamon
Sweetened whipped cream
Candy coffee beans

Combine wafer crumbs, melted butter, 1 tablespoon sugar and quarter-teaspoon cinnamon in a small bowl. Press evenly over bottom of a buttered 9″ springform pan. Refrigerate.

Beat cream cheese until smooth. Gradually beat in 1½ cups sugar; add eggs, one at a time, beating well. Stir in sour cream, liqueur, vanilla, whipping cream, melted chocolate and half-teaspoon cinnamon. Blend well. Pour into crust-lined pan. Bake at 325° for 1 hour and 15 minutes. Do not open oven door. Turn oven off and leave cheesecake in another hour. Remove and cool slightly, then refrigerate.

To serve, remove cake from pan. Garnish with sweetened whipped-cream rosettes, sprinkled lightly with cinnamon and topped with candy coffee beans. Makes 8 to 12 servings.

I'll Have Another Fruit Bar

Leslie Ann Posen

This "sweet thing" won the snacks category title in the 1984 Healthy Appetite contest for Leslie Ann Posen. You can choose any dried fruit you want to cover the bottom layer of the bar, which is full of what later became the favorite miracle food of 1989 — oats.

▼▼▼▼▼▼▼▼▼▼▼▼▼▼▼▼▼▼▼▼

2 cups rolled oats
2 cups whole wheat flour
3/4 cup butter or margarine,
  melted
1 cup honey, divided
3/4 teaspoon cinnamon
1/2 teaspoon cardamom
1/4 teaspoon salt or salt
  substitute
2 tablespoons fresh lemon
  juice

1 can (8 ounces) chunky
  applesauce, unsweetened
ANY FOUR OF THE
FOLLOWING:
1/2 cup chopped dates
1/2 cup chopped figs
1/2 cup golden raisins
1/2 cup raisins
1/2 cup chopped dried
  apricots
1/2 cup chopped dried
  pineapple

Preheat oven to 400°. Combine oats, flour, ½ cup honey, cinnamon, cardamom, salt and butter or margarine until crumbly. Press half the mixture into a greased 13" by 9" by 2" baking dish.

In saucepan, combine ½ cup honey and lemon juice. Add applesauce and dried fruit. Cook and stir over low heat about 10 minutes. Cool slightly and spread evenly over mixture in pan. Finely crumble remaining oat mixture over fruit. Bake at 400° for 20 to 25 minutes. Cut into bars. Makes 24 bars.

Candied Orange-Chocolate Cookies

Colleen T. Murphy

The contest theme for 1986, Festive Favorites, was one of the very best we ever had. Readers had to explain why their recipe was a "festive favorite." We published with each recipe the written quote from the contestant. Colleen T. Murphy of Phoenix said that her little boy especially enjoyed helping dip this family holiday favorite into the chocolate.

▼▼▼▼▼▼▼▼▼▼▼▼▼▼▼▼▼▼▼▼▼

1 cup butter or margarine,
   softened
1/2 cup sugar
1 large egg, lightly beaten
1 teaspoon vanilla extract
2 1/2 cups all-purpose flour

2 tablespoons grated orange
   peel
2 tablespoons sugar
1 package (6 ounces)
   semisweet chocolate chips

In large bowl with electric mixer at medium speed, beat butter, sugar, egg and vanilla until light and fluffy. Reduce speed to low, gradually beat in flour until just blended. If dough is too stiff, beat in 1 to 2 tablespoons of water. Shape dough into ball, wrap in plastic wrap and refrigerate at least 1 hour or up to 24 hours.

Preheat oven to 350°. Remove dough from refrigerator and roll out on lightly floured surface to ⅜" thickness. Cut dough into 1" wide strips; cut strips into 2" bars. Place bars about 1" apart on ungreased cookie sheet.

In small bowl, combine orange peel and 2 tablespoons sugar; sprinkle mixture over half of each cookie. Bake 10-12 minutes until firm; tops should be lightly colored and bottoms pale golden brown. Remove to wire racks to cool completely.

Meanwhile, in small saucepan over very low heat, melt chocolate chips, stirring constantly, until smooth. Dip plain half of each cookie into chocolate to coat; place on waxed paper until coating is set. Makes 5 dozen cookies.

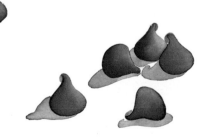

Perfect Pineapple Pound Mold

Pam Nelson

In 1983, Pam Nelson of Scottsdale almost won the best-of-contest prize with Perfect Pineapple Pound Mold, a show-stopper aptly entered in the Extravaganza category. This cake is baked in the shape of a pineapple, and decorated to look like one. Pineapple-lovers will flip: it also has pineapple in the batter and as a filling.

If you don't have a two-piece, egg-shaped mold and can't rent or borrow one from a friend, bake the pound-cake batter in loaf pans and carve it into pineapple shapes.

▼▼▼▼▼▼▼▼▼▼▼▼▼▼▼▼▼▼▼▼▼▼

1/2 cup shortening
1 cup margarine
2 3/4 cups sugar
6 large eggs
3 cups flour
1 teaspoon baking powder
1/4 cup milk
3/4 teaspoon vanilla
3/4 cup crushed pineapple,
   undrained
1 pineapple top (or greens to
   simulate top)
1/2 cup crushed pineapple,
   well-drained

Cream shortening, margarine and sugar until light and fluffy. Add
eggs, 1 at a time. Add flour and baking powder, 1 spoonful at a time
alternating with milk. Stir in vanilla and pineapple. Pour into
greased two-piece egg mold. Bake at 350° for 35 to 45 minutes.
Cool. Split into thirds and fill with well-drained pineapple. Frost
with fudge frosting (*recipe below*). Makes 12 servings.

FUDGE FROSTING:
1/2 cup butter
1/3 cup corn syrup
1/4 teaspoon salt

1 teaspoon vanilla
3/4 cup cocoa
1/3 cup milk
1 pound powdered sugar

Cream butter, corn syrup, salt and vanilla. Stir in cocoa. Add milk
and powdered sugar and beat well.

To decorate, use a star-tipped tube to cover the cake with stars,
to simulate the skin of a pineapple. (Alternately, frost cake and then
decorate with chocolate kisses.)

Margarita Pie

Roseann Kolicko

What's one of the first things people do when they move to Arizona?
They go to a Mexican restaurant and order a margarita. The elusive
sweet-salty flavor speedily becomes a favorite, as you can tell from
the proliferation of dishes in this cookbook that were based on that
tequila-Triple Sec-lime juice combination. The following, sent in by
Roseann Kolicko of Peoria for the 1982 Taste of Arizona Contest, has
several variations.

▼▼▼▼▼▼▼▼▼▼▼▼▼▼▼▼▼▼▼▼▼▼

1 9" graham cracker pie
shell (homemade or
prepared)
1 can (14 ounces) sweetened
condensed milk (not
evaporated milk)
1 1/2 ounces tequila
1 1/2 ounces Triple Sec

4 ounces fresh lime juice
(about 2 limes)
1 1/2 cups heavy cream,
stiffly beaten
GARNISH:
Whipped cream
Thin slices of lime

In a medium bowl, combine condensed milk, tequila and Triple Sec.
Add lime juice. Fold into whipped cream. Pour into pie shell and
freeze 4 to 5 hours. When ready to serve, garnish with more whipped
cream and thin slices of lime. Makes 8 servings.

Margarita Mousse

Art Blinick

This is another Zest of the Southwest creation, courtesy Art Blinick of Tempe. Art came up with a mousse margarita lovers will find familiar, flavored with lime juice, tequila and Triple Sec. The recipe for candied lime peel, the garnish, can be used for any kind of citrus. The finishing touch is serving this dessert in margarita glasses — minus the salt on the rim.

▼▼▼▼▼▼▼▼▼▼▼▼▼▼▼▼▼▼▼▼

**1/4 cup fresh lime juice
(unstrained)
2 tablespoons tequila
2 tablespoons Triple Sec
liqueur
1 packet unflavored gelatin
4 eggs, separated
1 cup sugar**

**1 cup whipping cream
CANDIED LIME PEEL:
4 limes
2 cups sugar
1 cup cold water
GARNISH:
Lime wedges**

In small bowl, combine lime juice, tequila and Triple Sec. Sprinkle gelatin on liquid and set aside to soften. Beat egg yolks, gradually adding ½ cup sugar, for 2 to 3 minutes until thick and pale yellow. Place yolk-sugar mixture in top of double boiler over simmering water.

Combine with gelatin mixture, whipping thoroughly with a whisk. Cook, stirring constantly, until thickened, about 5 minutes. Pour into a large bowl and refrigerate until it can be mounded, about 20 minutes.

Beat egg whites in a large bowl, until frothy. Gradually add the other ½ cup sugar, beating until glossy, stiff peaks are formed. Fold one-quarter of egg whites into the yolk mixture, then fold in the rest.

Beat cream until soft peaks are formed. Fold into the mousse. Chill 4 hours until set.

To make candied lime peel:

Peel rind of 4 limes. Slice into ⅛″ wide pieces, 1″ long. Drop into boiling water; boil uncovered for 10 minutes. Drain and rinse under cold water. Reserve. Combine 2 cups sugar and 1 cup cold water in medium saucepan. Bring to boiling, stirring to dissolve sugar.

Boil 5 minutes without stirring. Add lime rind and boil 15 minutes. Drain and let dry.

Serve mousse in margarita glasses, garnished with lime wedges and Candied Lime Peel. Makes 4 to 6 servings.

Potato Chip Cookies

Lorraine Lang

For every contest, the *Republic* corralled distinguished guests to judge the final dishes. The list of names through the years reads like a Who's Who of Valley food-dom. We had chefs, restaurant owners and managers, cooking teachers, nutritionists, restaurant consultants and movers and shakers in the Chef's Association of Greater Phoenix. The first panel we ever assembled, in 1981, gave this simple drop cookie high points for taste, ease of preparation, creativity and totability. (The theme was The Movable Feast.) Mesa resident Lorraine Lang almost won with it. The recipe has no eggs and resembles the popular Mexican Wedding Cookies, except it's even less trouble to make. Bet you can't eat just one!

▼▼▼▼▼▼▼▼▼▼▼▼▼▼▼▼▼▼▼▼▼

1 pound (4 sticks) butter or margarine
1 cup sugar
2 teaspoons vanilla
3 1/2 cups flour

4 ounces crushed potato chips (about 6 cups whole chips, crushed to make 3 cups)
1/2 cup nuts (optional)
Powdered sugar

With an electric mixer, cream butter and sugar until smooth. Add vanilla, flour, chips and nuts. Mix thoroughly. Drop from teaspoon onto ungreased cookie sheets. Bake in a pre-heated 350° oven for 15 to 20 minutes. When cool, sprinkle tops with powder sugar, using a sifter or strainer. Makes 8 to 9 dozen.

Arizona Date Pie

Peggy Yoder

The year was 1987 and three of the four desserts finalists were named Peggy. When she won the Desserts category in the Zest of the Southwest contest, Phoenix resident Peggy Yoder recalled growing up in Litchfield Park, where her mother made her climb the big, old date palms to pick fruit for this pie.

▼▼▼▼▼▼▼▼▼▼▼▼▼▼▼▼▼▼▼

1/2 cup butter or margarine	1/2 cup chopped pecans
1 cup sugar	1 cup chopped dates
3 eggs, lightly beaten	1 (9") unbaked pie shell
3/4 cup dark corn syrup	GARNISH:
1/4 teaspoon salt	Whipped cream
1 teaspoon vanilla	8 dates stuffed with cream cheese

In a large bowl of an electric mixer, cream together butter and sugar until light and fluffy. Add eggs, corn syrup, salt, vanilla, pecans and chopped dates. Blend well. Pour into pastry shell.

Bake on lower shelf of oven at 375° for 40 to 45 minutes. Top with whipped cream; decorate with stuffed dates. Makes 8 to 12 servings.

Eggless, Milkless Cake

Muriel Prigge

Muriel Prigge's version of an oldie-but-goodie cropped up in the 1984 Healthy Appetites contest. Ironically, this hard-times favorite, concocted by thrifty cooks when richer ingredients were scarce, is right at home in today's cholesterol-free kitchens.

▼▼▼▼▼▼▼▼▼▼▼▼▼▼▼▼▼▼▼

2 cups sugar	1/2 teaspoon cloves
1/2 cup all-vegetable shortening	1/2 teaspoon allspice
2 cups boiling water	1 teaspoon cinnamon
2 cups raisins	Pinch salt
1 cup cold water	1 teaspoon baking powder
1 tablespoon baking soda	1 teaspoon vanilla
4 cups flour	3/4 cup chopped nuts

Preheat oven to 350°. In a large mixing bowl, cream together sugar and shortening. In a medium saucepan, pour the 2 cups boiling water over the raisins and simmer 15 minutes. Remove from heat, add the 1 cup cold water, and allow to cool. When cool, add the baking soda. Stir raisin mixture into sugar-and-shortening mixture.

Sift dry ingredients into raisin mixture and stir only enough to moisten. Stir in vanilla and nuts. Pour into two greased 1-pound loaf pans. Bake at 350° for 1 hour. Makes 12 to 24 servings.

Threshers

Gwen Gurule

Another favorite from the 1986 Festive Favorites contest. This is a great recipe to use up small amounts of cereal left in big boxes. Gwen Gurule of Sun City wrote, "I invented Threshers to get more whole grains into our diet since we weren't big cereal eaters. We'd eat handfuls of them while digging live Christmas trees in the snowy mountain forests. My husband and his brothers were so enthusiastic about them, I began including them in my holiday gift assortments. They became my single most universally successful cookie recipe."

▼▼▼▼▼▼▼▼▼▼▼▼▼▼▼▼▼▼▼▼

1/2 cup vegetable oil
1 cup honey
2 eggs
1/4 cup milk
1 tablespoon coffee liqueur
   or 1 teaspoon vanilla
1 2/3 cups flour (whole
   wheat, unbleached white,
   or a blend)
1 1/2 teaspoon baking
   powder
1/2 teaspoon salt

1 teaspoon cinnamon
1 teaspoon ginger
1/2 teaspoon nutmeg
1/2 teaspoon cardamom
1/4 teaspoon cloves
2 cups cereal (any combination of bran, cornmeal,
   oats, any uncooked hot
   cereal or cold cereal of
   your choice)
1 cup raisins
1 cup chopped nuts
1 cup chocolate chips

Preheat oven to 375°. Combine oil and honey in a large mixing bowl. Blend in eggs, milk and liqueur or vanilla. Add flour mixed with baking powder, salt and spices. Mix thoroughly. Add cereals, mixing well after each addition. Stir in raisins, nuts and chocolate chips. Put spoonfuls of dough 2″ apart on greased cookie sheets. Bake 10 to 12 minutes at 375°. Makes 4 to 5 dozen cookies.

Orange Daydreamer Surprise

Michele Broadbent

This was the grand prize winner in the second recipe contest, 1983's Just Desserts. Michele Broadbent came from Provo, Utah, for the contest, and went home with $500. (Her mother in Mesa had sent her a Food section with the entry blank.) Michelle used Arizona flavors—oranges, pecans and raisins—in her unusual dessert sandwich. She suggested serving this hearty, sweet cousin to the French *croque-monsieur* for brunch or after a football game. (You could also quarter the sandwiches into triangles before battering.)

▼▼▼▼▼▼▼▼▼▼▼▼▼▼▼▼▼▼▼

FILLING:
1 package (8 ounces) cream cheese
1/3 cup chopped pecans
1 tablespoon orange juice
1/2 teaspoon grated orange peel
10 slices raisin-cinnamon bread
BATTER:
1 cup flour
2 1/2 teaspoons sugar
2 teaspoons baking powder
1 teaspoon salt
1 cup half-and-half
2 eggs, beaten
Oil for frying
ORANGE SYRUP:
2 cups orange juice
1 1/2 cups sugar
3 teaspoons grated orange peel
1/4 teaspoon nutmeg
1 teaspoon ground cinnamon
3 large oranges, peeled and sectioned
Cornstarch (optional)

In medium mixing bowl, combine cream cheese, pecans, orange juice and orange peel. Blend until smooth. Spread on bread to make 5 sandwiches.

In a medium bowl, combine flour, sugar, baking powder and salt. Beat in half-and-half and beaten eggs to form a smooth batter. Heat 3" to 4" of oil in a deep-fat fryer to 375°. Dip sandwiches in batter to coat both sides. Fry until lightly brown; turn and fry other side. Remove and drain on paper towels.

To make orange sauce:

In a small saucepan, combine orange juice, sugar, orange peel, nutmeg and cinnamon. Stir over low heat until sugar dissolves. Thicken with a little cornstarch, if desired. Remove from heat. Add orange sections. Serve hot over Orange Daydreamer Surprise. Makes 5 servings.

Baked Bananas

Candace Unglesby

Tempe reader Candace Unglesby invented this recipe just after she
got out of college, and often made it to serve hot over ice cream.
It so impressed the judges in the 1983 Just Desserts contest that
she was named the winner in the Last-Minute Desserts category.
Once it is put together in a baking dish, it needs no further turning,
stirring, or other attention. The ingredients are easy to keep on
hand, so it can truly be a last-minute winner in your kitchen, too.
(To make it even faster: heat the apricot preserves in the microwave
to melt them; then zap the sauced bananas on medium-high for 3
to 4 minutes, stirring once or twice.)

▼▼▼▼▼▼▼▼▼▼▼▼▼▼▼▼▼▼▼

4 ripe bananas
1 jar (6 to 8 ounces) apricot
  preserves

1/2 cup fresh orange juice
1/4 cup rum
Coconut

Peel bananas and place in 8″ by 8″ glass baking dish. Heat apricot
preserves and stir in juice and rum. Pour over bananas, sprinkle
with coconut.

Bake at 350° for 25 minutes. Serve warm. Fabulous over ice
cream. Makes 4 servings.

Frozen Raspberry Macadamia Dessert

Pamela Jackson

Pamela Jackson's experience entering recipes in contests was one shared by many: she waited until the last minute. On the final day recipe entries were accepted, Pamela dropped four into a 1988 Easy Entertaining collection box—to do this, she had to go out in a downpour that set a record in the Valley for one-day rainfall. The drenching the Tempe resident got was worth it, she decided, when she won the desserts category with this easy recipe, which features a nut crust and a base of sweetened condensed milk.

▼▼▼▼▼▼▼▼▼▼▼▼▼▼▼▼▼▼▼▼

CRUST:
1 cup (20 wafers) crushed
vanilla wafers
1/2 cup finely chopped
macadamia nuts
(or almonds)
1/4 cup margarine or butter,
melted
FILLING:
1 can (14 ounces) sweetened
condensed milk (not
evaporated)

3 tablespoons lemon juice
3 tablespoons orange-
flavored liqueur or
orange juice
1 package (10 ounces) frozen
raspberries with syrup,
thawed
1 cup whipping cream,
whipped
GARNISH:
Additional whipping cream
Chocolate shavings

Heat oven to 375°. In a small bowl, combine all crust ingredients and mix well. Press mixture firmly in the bottom of an 8″ springform pan. Bake for 8 to 10 minutes. Cool.

In large bowl, combine condensed milk, lemon juice and liqueur or orange juice; beat until smooth. Add raspberries and beat at low speed until well-blended. Fold in whipped cream.

Pour over cooled crust. Freeze until firm. Remove 15 minutes before serving time and let stand at room temperature. Garnish with whipped cream and chocolate shavings. Makes 12 servings.

Coffee-Nut Tortoni

Ann Reque

This elegant, very simple creation took the prize in the Family Traditions division of the Just Desserts contest in 1983. The nuts and coconut add texture to the tortoni's smooth richness. Ann Reque of Scottsdale said, "I started making Coffee Nut Tortoni when my two sons were very small. It became our family's favorite dessert. Now both boys are grown, and they make the tortoni themselves, especially when they entertain."

▼▼▼▼▼▼▼▼▼▼▼▼▼▼▼▼▼▼▼▼▼

1 cup whipping cream
1/4 cup sugar
1 tablespoon instant coffee
powder
1 teaspoon vanilla
Few drops almond extract
1 egg white
2 tablespoons sugar

1/4 cup flaked coconut,
toasted and crumbled
1/4 cup almonds, finely
chopped and toasted
GARNISH:
Maraschino cherries
(optional)

Whip cream, fold in ¼ cup sugar, instant coffee, vanilla and almond extract. In a small bowl, combine coconut and almonds.

Beat egg white until soft peaks form. Fold in 2 tablespoons sugar and beat to stiff peaks.

Mix half the nut mixture into the whipped cream. Fold egg white into the whipped cream.

Spoon into 8 souffle cups or custard cups. Sprinkle remaining nut mixture over tops of servings.

Set dishes on small tray. Place in freezer. Just before serving, top each with a maraschino cherry. Makes 8 servings.

Prickly Pear Cheesecake

Peggy Milholland

Scottsdale's Peggy Milholland developed this cheesecake for a
Mexican-theme potluck at work, using prickly pear jelly and piñon
nuts. With its red-glazed top, the pie won high marks from the 1987
Zest of the Southwest judges.

▼▼▼▼▼▼▼▼▼▼▼▼▼▼▼▼▼▼▼

CRUST:
2 cups crushed graham
   cracker crumbs
2 1/2 tablespoons sugar
1/2 cup melted butter
1/2 cup piñon (pine) nuts,
   finely chopped
FILLING:
4 packages (8 ounces each)
   cream cheese, softened
1 1/2 cups sugar
4 eggs

1 1/2 teaspoons vanilla
1 cup sour cream
1 cup whipping cream
1/4 teaspoon lemon juice
2/3 cup prickly pear
   preserves
Whipped cream for topping
   (optional)
GLAZE:
1 cup prickly pear jelly
2 tablespoons Grand Marnier

To make crust:
   Mix graham cracker crumbs, sugar, butter and nuts together.
Press firmly on the bottom and sides of a 9" springform pan. Chill.

To make filling:
   With an electric mixer, cream together cream cheese and sugar
until smooth. Add 1 egg at a time, beating well; blend in vanilla.
By hand, add sour cream, whipping cream and lemon juice.

   Pour half this mixture into the crust. Spoon half the preserves
over the batter. Add remaining batter and repeat with remaining
preserves. Swirl with a knife for a marbled effect. Bake at 325° for
1 hour and 15 minutes. Turn oven off and leave in oven 1 hour.
Remove from oven and let cool. Chill overnight.

   For glaze, melt jelly and Grand Marnier over low heat. Pour atop
chilled cheesecake. Spread evenly and let set. Decorate edges with
whipped cream piping. Makes 8 to 12 servings.

Bingo Bars

Virjean Svoboda

As far as I can determine, this is the only winning recipe in all our contests that contained baby food! Virjean Svoboda of Scottsdale took home the cash in the desserts category for her Bingo Bars, which she entered in the first contest, 1981's Movable Feast. Svoboda was one of the first people to congratulate the grand prize winner that year, Laurel Thompson. The two women worked together in a Scottsdale orthodontist's office, but neither knew the other had entered until they both received phone calls telling them they were finalists.

▼▼▼▼▼▼▼▼▼▼▼▼▼▼▼▼▼▼▼▼▼

3 eggs
2 cups sugar
1 1/4 cups vegetable oil
2 cups flour
2 teaspoons cinnamon
2 teaspoons soda
1 small jar (2 1/2 ounces) strained apricot baby food

1 small jar (2 1/2 ounces) strained applesauce baby food
1 small jar (2 1/2 ounces) strained carrots baby food
1 cup chopped pecans (optional)
Icing (*recipe follows*)

Preheat oven to 350°. In a large mixing bowl, beat eggs and gradually add sugar. Mix well. Add salad oil and blend. Sift together the dry ingredients. Combine baby foods in a bowl; alternately add dry ingredients and baby food to egg-sugar mixture. Stir in pecans if using. Bake in greased and floured 10" by 15" jellyroll pan for 25 to 30 minutes at 350°.
Makes 50 1" by 3" bars.

ICING:
2 packages (3 ounces each)
cream cheese
6 tablespoons margarine

1 teaspoon vanilla
1 tablespoon cream or milk
1/4 teaspoon salt
4 cups powdered sugar

Cream margarine and cream cheese; add vanilla, cream or milk, salt and powdered sugar. Beat until light and fluffy and spread on bars.

Dessert Tostada with Lime Cream

Peggy Milholland

Scottsdale's Peggy Milholland made a habit out of entering our recipe contests. And her sister did the same thing (see recipes, pages 99 and 107). This was Milholland's 1988 Easy Entertaining entry. She didn't place as a finalist, but she came to the contest at Metro-Center to cheer on her sister, who made Cheesy Seafood Lasagna Rolls in the Buffets category. This recipe teaches a couple of useful things: how to make tortilla baskets and lime curd. Both are useful, versatile skills. You can fill the tortilla baskets with anything, sweet or savory, and the lime curd is delicious as a spread for toast, filling for pound cake, etc. All the different parts to this dessert can be made a day or two ahead of time and assembled quickly at the last minute.

▼▼▼▼▼▼▼▼▼▼▼▼▼▼▼▼▼▼▼

6 flour tortillas (7″ to 8″ in
diameter)
Oil
3/4 cup whipping cream

1 cup lime curd (*recipe
***follows*)**
3 tablespoons semisweet
chocolate curls
Fresh strawberries

In a deep 4-quart pan, heat 1½″ salad oil to 375°. Float 1 tortilla on top of the oil. With the bowl of a metal ladle, press down on the center of the tortilla until it touches the bottom of the pan and oil bubbles up around the tortilla. Hold tortilla down until it is a golden brown, about 2 minutes. Lift from oil with tongs and a slotted spoon and drain over pan. Let cool and drain on paper towels. Repeat to cook the remaining tortillas. (If made the night before, store in airtight container.)

In a small bowl, beat whipping cream to soft peaks. In another bowl, stir lime curd until smooth; fold into whipped cream. Use, or cover and chill overnight.

Place tortillas on dessert plates; spoon about one-third cup of the lime curd mixture into each. Sprinkle with chocolate and garnish with strawberries. To eat, break off chunks of the tortilla to scoop through filling. Makes 6 servings.

LIME CURD:

4 to 5 limes	1 cup sugar
1 egg	4 tablespoons unsalted
3 egg yolks	butter, cut into pieces

Remove green skin (zest) from 2 of the limes. Scrape off any bitter white pith left on the zest. Place the zest in a small saucepan. Add enough boiling water to cover and blanch over high heat for 1 minute. Drain and pat dry on paper towels. Finely chop the zest.

Halve and squeeze enough of the limes to produce ½ cup lime juice. In a small bowl, beat together the whole egg and egg yolks. In a small, heavy saucepan (non-aluminum), combine the lime juice, zest and sugar. Stir to partially dissolve the sugar. Add the egg mixture and the butter. Cook over low heat, stirring until the mixture thickens enough to coat the back of a spoon, about 20 minutes. Do not let the mixture boil. It will thicken as it cools. Strain the curd into a clean, dry heatproof jar, cover with waxed paper and cool. Cover the jar and refrigerate until chilled. Keeps very well if refrigerated.

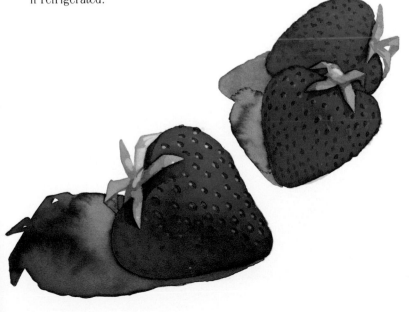

Adobe Pinto Torte

Margaret Rhodes

Margaret "Peg" Rhodes of Prescott developed this recipe for our Healthy Appetites contest in 1984, and it nearly stole the grand prize. Judges loved the flavor, the originality and the bonus of the nutritional boost from the main ingredient: *frijoles*. Unseasoned pinto beans add fiber (the soluble kind found in apples and oat bran), complex carbohydrates and moisture. Plus, this is one of those great recipes you can serve to unsupecting friends—and let them try to guess the main ingredient. Peg said she came up with the idea when she began to make her pumpkin torte recipe and found she was out of canned pumpkin.

▼▼▼▼▼▼▼▼▼▼▼▼▼▼▼▼▼▼▼▼▼

1/4 cup corn oil margarine
1/4 cup molasses
1/4 cup unsweetened
  applesauce
1 egg
2 egg whites
2 cups cooked pinto beans,
  unseasoned and drained
  (1 1/4 cups mashed or
  pureed)
1 1/3 cups whole wheat flour
1 teaspoon baking soda
1 teaspoon cinnamon

1/2 teaspoon ground cloves
1/2 teaspoon ground
  allspice
2 cups tart apple, finely diced
1/2 cup dates or other dried
  fruit, finely chopped
1/2 cup pecans, finely
  chopped
1 teaspoon vanilla extract
1/2 teaspoon lemon extract
Pecan halves
Low-sugar apple jelly, melted

Preheat oven to 375°. Lightly grease two 9″ cake pans or one 9″ tube pan. In a medium bowl, beat together with an electric mixer the margarine, molasses, egg, egg whites and applesauce. Beat in mashed beans. Set aside.

Sift together flour, baking soda, cinnamon, cloves and allspice. Add to bean mixture and beat well. Stir in apple, dates, nuts and vanilla and lemon extracts. Pour into greased pan. Bake at 375° for 40 to 45 minutes or until center tests done with a toothpick. If using a tube pan, bake 45 to 55 minutes or until done.

Cool 10 minutes in pan. Gently remove rim of pan and allow torte to finish cooling on wire rack. Meanwhile, heat apple jelly in small saucepan. Glaze top of warm torte with melted jelly and arrange pecan halves as desired. Cut into wedges. Makes 2 tortes or one cake.

Elegant Cantaloupe Granita

Terry Danielsen

The simplicity of this dish does not make it any less elegant. It comes from the 1984 Healthy Appetites contest, and Terry Danielsen's entry is especially refreshing on a muggy August day in Phoenix. You Valley residents know the kind of day I'm talking about....You hear yourself say, "Oh, it's only going to be 104° today," and then realize that you really mean it!

▼▼▼▼▼▼▼▼▼▼▼▼▼▼▼▼▼▼▼▼▼

2 large, ripe cantaloupes
1/4 cup honey
1 cup water

1/2 cup sauterne (or white
   grape juice)
GARNISH:
Fresh mint leaves

Heat honey and water, stirring constantly, until honey is dissolved. Cool. Slice canteloupes into quarters. Remove seeds and pulp, chopping pulp into small pieces.

Place shells in freezer. Place canteloupe pulp and sauterne in bowl. Combine honey-water mixture with canteloupe and sauterne. Pour into freezing trays (or a metal 8″ by 8″ pan) and freeze until crystals form around the edges. Break up mixture with a fork. Repeat about four times an hour until little ice grains have formed. Spoon cantaloupe granita into frozen shells and garnish with sprigs of fresh mint. Makes 8 servings.

Chocolate Applesauce Cake

Margaret Arcieri

This is my idea of a near-perfect cake recipe. It's chocolate, it goes together in just a few minutes and it's attractive even without frosting. My sister-in-law, Vera Walker, tested this contribution from Scottsdale's Margaret Arcieri to the 1981 Movable Feast contest; Vera said that if she can make it and have it turn out as well as it did, anybody can. (Vera used sliced almonds on top of the cake. Lovely.)

▼▼▼▼▼▼▼▼▼▼▼▼▼▼▼▼▼▼▼

1/2 cup margarine
1 3/4 cups sugar
2 cups applesauce
2 eggs
2 cups flour
1/2 teaspoon cinnamon
3 tablespoons cocoa

1 1/2 teaspoons baking soda
1/2 teaspoon salt
TOPPING:
3 tablespoons sugar
1/2 cup chopped nuts
1 bag (6 ounces) chocolate
   chips

Preheat oven to 350°. In a large mixing bowl, cream margarine with sugar. Add applesauce, eggs, flour, cinnamon, cocoa, salt and baking soda. Mix and pour into a greased 13″ by 9″ pan. Sprinkle chocolate chips, nuts and 3 tablespoons sugar over the top of cake. Bake at 350° for 35 to 40 minutes. Makes 12 servings.

Grandma Pryor's Butterscotch Refrigerator Cookies

Ernie Startup

Ernie Startup of Phoenix writes a beautiful recipe (check out the Sinkers in the breads chapter to see what I mean). Here's another one, from the year of Festive Favorites, 1986, the year we asked people to explain why their recipe was a favorite. Here is (much abbreviated, unfortunately) Ernie's explanation: "For as long as I can remember Christmas, I can remember eating Grandma Pryor's Butterscotch Ice Box Cookies, and I'm old enough to collect Social Security. I'll never forget the first time we made them together. I must have been five or six. She measured exactly—Grandma Pryor did everything exactly—enough butter into an even bigger crock...

While we worked, Grandma explained that she got the recipe from her mother who had died when she was fourteen, and although you could get baking powder, it wasn't the same as the cream of tartar and soda together, and although you could get waxed paper, she still preferred to butter a piece of cheesecloth to make it airtight to wrap around the cookies while they melted overnight....So I must have eaten these cookies for at least 65 Christmases. This year, for the first time, I have a grandson to make them for."

▼▼▼▼▼▼▼▼▼▼▼▼▼▼▼▼▼▼▼▼▼

1 cup butter	**5 cups flour**
4 cups light brown sugar	**1 tablespoon baking soda**
4 extra-large eggs	**1 tablespoon cream of tartar**
2 teaspoons vanilla	**4 cups pecan meats**

In large bowl of mixer, cream butter. Gradually add sugar. Cream to color and consistency of thick cream. Add eggs 1 at a time, beating well after each addition. Add vanilla.

Sift flour, baking soda and cream of tartar together; mix into butter, sugar and egg mixture with wooden spoon. Add nuts. Form into 1″ rolls and wrap in plastic wrap. Store in refrigerator at least overnight. Slice in ¼″ slices and put well apart on very lightly greased cookie sheet. These cookies spread to more than twice their size. Bake in preheated 275° oven 10 to 12 minutes, until nicely brown.

If well-wrapped in plastic, the cookie dough can be kept as long as 6 weeks in the refrigerator, or longer in the freezer. Have a pan baking or freshly out of the oven as guests arrive at Christmas time, and the house smells like Christmas. Makes 10 to 12 dozen cookies.

Our Honey-Yogurt Cheesecake

Deborah Howard

This is a real tempter, from Phoenix resident Deborah Howard for the 1983 Just Desserts contest. It was the first time I ever tasted a cheesecake that contained yogurt. Can you believe that this now-universal ingredient was considered unusual in 1983?

▼▼▼▼▼▼▼▼▼▼▼▼▼▼▼▼▼▼▼▼

CRUST:
1 3/4 cups graham cracker
  crumbs
1/3 cup walnuts, finely
  chopped
1 teaspoon cinnamon
1/2 cup butter or margarine,
  melted
FILLING:
3 eggs

2 packages (8 ounces each)
  cream cheese, softened
1/2 cup honey
2 teaspoons vanilla
2 to 3 teaspoons fresh lemon
  juice
1 cup plain yogurt
2 cups sour cream
1 pint strawberries (or
  favorite fruit)
1/2 cup liqueur

Preheat oven to 375°. Combine graham cracker crumbs, nuts, cinnamon and butter. Spread into a 9″ springform pan. Press onto bottom and up sides.

Soak strawberries in liqueur. Set aside. In a medium mixing bowl, beat eggs, cream cheese, honey, vanilla and lemon juice until smooth. Blend in yogurt and sour cream. Pour into crust. Bake at 375° for 35 minutes or until set. Cool and chill for 4 to 5 hours.

At time of serving, arrange strawberries decoratively around the top. Drizzle the remaining liqueur over berries. Makes 14 servings.

Arizona Pecan Lemon Cake

Joan Griffiths

I love lemons, so this became a personal favorite the first time I made it. If you love lemons, you, too, will adore this cake, which is similar to a pound cake. It is even better the second day after it's made. (*Note:* This is a heavy batter, and a stationary or heavy-duty mixer is a must. Try it with a hand mixer at your own risk!) Joan Griffiths of Mesa entered the recipe in the Zest of the Southwest contest in 1987.

4 cups all-purpose flour
1 teaspoon baking powder
1 pound butter
2 cups sugar
6 large eggs, separated
Grated rind of one lemon
1/2 cup fresh lemon juice

1 package (15 or 16 ounces,
or 2 1/2 cups) white
raisins
3 cups (12 ounces) chopped
Arizona pecans, lightly
toasted
1/8 teaspoon cream of tartar
1/2 cup white corn syrup
(optional)

Preheat oven to 275°. Have all ingredients at room temperature for greatest volume. Sift flour and baking powder together. Cream butter in large mixing bowl of stationary electric mixer. Gradually add sugar and continue creaming until light and fluffy.

Add egg yolks one at a time, beating well. Add grated lemon rind. Add flour mixture and creamed butter alternately with lemon juice, beginning and ending with flour. Fold in raisins and pecans. Batter will be very stiff.

In a separate bowl, add cream of tartar to egg whites and beat until stiff. Pour half of egg whites into batter. Using a large rubber spatula, fold in gently. Then fold in other half.

Pour batter into a 10" tube or Bundt pan coated with nonstick cooking spray. Bake 2 to 2½ hours in 275° oven or until cake tests done and is lightly browned. Glaze by pouring syrup over the top and spreading with spatula before the last 5 minutes of baking. (This last step is optional).

Remove to rack and let cool thoroughly before removing from pan. Invert on serving plate. Keeps well. Makes 12 to 16 servings.

INDEX

Judy Hille Walker had the good fortune to be born into a family of Okies who love to cook and eat. Raised in Perryville, Arkansas, she has a degree in English and journalism. She has been a writer all her life and a newspaper reporter for twelve years, ten of them with *The Arizona Republic*. From 1985 to 1989, she was food editor, until the food sections of the *Republic* and the *Phoenix Gazette* merged. Now Walker writes for the *Republic's* Features department, specializing in stories for Home and On the Go and Sun Living.

She is married to Dave Walker, who is also a feature writer and has a large following as Cap'n Dave, the fast-food reviewer for *New Times*, a Phoenix alternative weekly. They have one son, Mack, who was born at the same time as this cookbook.

Share a cookbook with a friend...

ANNIE'S BABYCAKES
By Anne Yohn

For cheesecake lovers
72 pages, $9.95

COWBOY COOKING
Compiled by Tom Watson

For the cowboy
at heart
172 pages, $14.95

**DE GRAZIA AND
MEXICAN COOKERY**
Recipes by Rita Davenport

Attractive guide to south-
of-the-border cooking
86 pages, $12.95

**THE LOST
NORWEGIAN**
by Christin Drake

Sumptuous
208 pages, $27.95

SAVORY SOUTHWEST
by Judy Hille Walker

Full of flavor, not fire
144 pages, $12.95

Enclosed is my check or money order for $ _____

Please Charge my ___ VISA ___ MC

Card number _____ Exp.date _____

Signature _____

Ship to _____

Address _____

City _____ State _____ ZIP _____

Description	COST	QTY	TOTAL
Annie's Babycakes	9.95		
Cowboy Cooking	14.95		
De Grazia and Mexican Cookery	12.95		
Lost Norwegian	27.95		
Savory Southwest	12.95		

Postage and Handling Chart			
		Sub-Total	
Under $10.00	$2.50	5.1% Sales Tax (AZ residents only)	
$10-24.99	$3.00	Postage and Handling	
Over $25.00	$3.75	Grand Total	

Ship order form and
payment information to :

Northland Publishing
P.O. Box 1389, Flagstaff, Arizona 86002
Or, for your convenience, please call us toll-free **1-800-346-3257**